Contents

Preface

How it all began

The Changing Days project started in December 1994 after a national consultation exercise which concluded that development of day opportunities for people with learning difficulties was a priority. The three-year project has been a partnership between the King's Fund and the National Development Team with funding from the Gatsby Charitable Foundation and the Joseph Rowntree Foundation.

The work is based on the belief that:

- people with learning disabilities have the ability to become full members of their local communities;
- better daytime opportunities can be achieved by working in partnership with users, carers and staff in planning and shaping the future;
- the future for people with learning difficulties should be away from segregated day centres and building-based services towards being given support to participate in ordinary activities in the community;
- the emphasis should be on developing adult education, employment and meaningful leisure pursuits outside segregated services. (*Changing Days*, 1996)

How we worked

We worked with five development sites who had demonstrated their commitment to develop services in this way:

Cambridgeshire County Council Social Services, 18–20 Signet Court, Swans Road, Cambridge CB5 8LA. Tel: 01223 718 448; fax: 01223 718 012

Ely Hospital, Cardiff Community Healthcare Trust, Cowbridge Road West, Ely, Cardiff CF5 5XE. Tel: 01222 562 323; fax: 01222 578 717

Hackney Social Services, 205 Morning Lane, London E9 6JX. Tel: 0181 986 3123; fax: 0181 533 0824

Hereford Single Agency Purchasing Project, Social Services Department, County Offices, Bath Street, Hereford HR1 2HQ. Tel: 01432 352 211; fax: 01432 363 062

South East Belfast Health & Social Services Trust, Knockbracken Healthcare Park, Saintfield Road, Belfast BT8 8BH. Tel: 01232 565 555; fax: 01232 565 813

Five action learning sets, administered by the National Development Team, met throughout the project. These provided the opportunity for a much wider range of managers and others to meet regularly to discuss issues around their own day services and work towards solutions. We are grateful to the following NDT consultants who facilitated the action learning sets: Peter Allen, Roger Blunden, Barbara McIntosh, Ann O'Bryan and Paul Taylor.

In addition, we met and worked with many other people, through conferences and working groups, by telephone and written contacts from all of whom we learned much about the current challenges facing people working in day services. The sometimes overwhelming numbers of enquiries from people seeking information and advice and wanting to share their ideas indicates the enormous amount of work going on and the diverse ways people are striving to create better day opportunities for the people they serve.

Linking with *Changing Days*

The first publication of the project, *Changing Days*, brought together current ideas and practice on how best to achieve the aims of the project. *Days of Change* builds on those ideas and reflects our own and other colleagues' experience of such working over the past two years.

We have deliberately tried to link the two books, as much of the material in *Changing Days* is still very relevant two years on. For example, the values and principles on which services should be based and the key issues arising out of that have not changed. Certain areas given special chapters in *Changing Days* are not repeated in this book (e.g. legal issues, accessible environments). The material in the chapter on minority ethnic groups in *Changing Days* should underpin all services: in this publication we have addressed those issues interwoven in various chapters.

We feel it is important that the two books are used together in order to cover all aspects of working to improve day opportunities.

Readership

Like *Changing Days* this book is written particularly for managers, commissioners and providers who are responsible for developing day opportunities for men and women with learning difficulties. However, it is designed to be helpful also to anyone involved in supporting people to improve their lives, including people who use services and their families.

Suggestions on how to use this book

Days of Change begins with an easy-to-read summary. Each chapter focuses on a specific area with emphasis on giving practical suggestions to managers and others in a position to make change happen. We do not suggest that you try to read it from cover to cover! This is a book for dipping into according to need. With this in mind, there is some repetition of key principles and practices which we feel is necessary for clarity. In most cases, the chapters have the same headings as those in *Changing Days*. We hope that the index will also make reference easier.

The terms 'learning difficulties' and 'learning disabilities' are used interchangeably.

The future

People with complex needs often seem to have the longest journey to travel before they become valued members of their community. Frustration expressed by staff and our own observations of the lack of opportunities for this group of people has led us to set up a new programme. Funding from TSB Lloyds will enable us to work over the next two years, focusing specifically on people who have high support needs. Our aim will be to demonstrate good practice in developing and implementing improved day opportunities across health, social services and the independent sector.

For some men and women with learning difficulties, positive change is already happening in their lives. The key challenge is to make it happen for everyone. We hope this book will be a catalyst for further progress.

Barbara McIntosh
Andrea Whittaker
Changing Days Team

Acknowledgements

This book has come about through the combined efforts of all the contributors listed on pages ix–xii. We are grateful to all these people for contributing their time and experience. Without their help the book could not have been written.

We want to thank also all the people in the development sites we got to know so well during the past two years – people with learning difficulties, their parents and carers and staff at all levels of the service.

Particular thanks go to Simon Whitehead, Deputy Director of the National Development Team, and Janice Robinson, Director of the Community Care Programme at the King's Fund, for their advisory role.

Thanks also to Giovanna Ceroni, Managing Editor, Minuche Mazumdar, Design Manager, Linda Moore for her administrative and word-processing support, and Peter and Matt Powell for typesetting this volume.

Contributors

Service change/redesign

Roger Blunden   Ty Coch, Llanfihangel, Llanfyllin, Powys, SY22 5JD.
Tel: 01691 648 909

Angela Cole   Freelance Consultant (formerly Hackney Social Services)

Louanne Hempton   South & East Belfast Health & Social Services Trust, Trust HQ,
Knockbracken Healthcare Park, Saintfield Road, Belfast BT8 8BH.
Tel: 01232 790 673

Ann Lloyd   The Community Resource Service, 55 Albion Grove, London N16 8RE.
Tel: 0171 923 0200

Barbara McIntosh   Project Manager, Changing Days, King's Fund,
11–13 Cavendish Square, London W1M 0AN. Tel: 0171 307 2647

Simon Whitehead   Deputy Director, National Development Team, St Peter's Court,
8 Trumpet Street, Manchester M1 5LW. Tel: 0161 228 7055

Strategic planning and commissioning

Peter Kinsella   24 Brancote Road, Oxton, Wirral, Merseyside. Tel: 0151 250 3000

Creating inclusive communities

Jim Bettridge   'Drws Agored', 12 Richards Terrace, Roath, Cardiff, CF2 1RU.
Tel: 01222 226 260

Christine Burke   London Mencap, 115 Golden Lane, London EC1Y OTJ.
Tel: 0171 696 5574.

Tomasz Dukanovitch   Manager, Community Support Team, Hackney Independent
Living Team, Martello House, Martello Street, London E8.
Tel: 0181 923 4444

Andrew Holman   Waldare, The Street, Herringswell, Bury-St-Edmunds IP28 6ST.
Tel: 01638 751 806

Andrea Whittaker   Project Officer, King's Fund, 11–13 Cavendish Square, London
W1M 0AN. Tel: 0171 307 2646

Transition and further education

Joan Maughan   Laundry Cottage, Laundry Lane, Thornham Magna I, Suffolk IP23 8GH.
Tel: 01379 783 858

Kevin McMullen   Sawston College, New Road, Sawston, Cambridge CB2 4BP.
Tel: 01223 832 217

Jeannie Sutcliffe   Development Officer, National Institute for Adult & Continuing
Education, 21 De Montfort Street, Leicester LE1 7GE.
Tel: 0116 255 1451

Supported employment

Steve Beyer   Deputy Director, Welsh Centre for Learning Disabilities,
Meridian Court, North Road, Cardiff CF4 3BL. Tel: 01222 691 795

People with complex disabilities

Andrew Holman   Waldare, The Street, Herringswell, Bury-St-Edmunds IP28 6ST.
Tel: 01638 751 806

John Ladle   Acting Up, 90 De Beauvoir Road, London N1 4EN. Tel: 0171 275 9173

Ann Lloyd   The Community Resource Service, 55 Albion Grove, London N16 8RE.
Tel: 0171 923 0200

Barbara McIntosh   Project Manager, Changing Days, King's Fund, 11–13 Cavendish
Square, London W1M 0AN. Tel: 0171 307 2647

Planning for individuals

Andrea Whittaker   Project Officer, King's Fund, 11–13 Cavendish Square, London
W1M 0AN. Tel: 0171 307 2646

Health care in the community

Margaret Flynn 1 Thorn Villas, Jumps Road, Lydgate, Todmorden, Lancs OL14 8HL.
Tel: 01706 819 291

Barbara McIntosh Project Manager, Changing Days, King's Fund, 11–13 Cavendish
Square, London W1M 0AN. Tel: 0171 307 2647

Parents/carers

Andrea Whittaker Project Officer, King's Fund, 11–13 Cavendish Square, London
W1M 0AN. Tel: 0171 307 2646

Resettlement

Tracey Anderson Ely Hospital, Cowbridge Road West, Ely, Cardiff CF5 5XE.
Tel: 01222 562 323

Tina Donovan Project Manager, Learning Disabilities, Bro Tas Health Authority,
Temple of Peace, Cathays Park, Cardiff CF1 3NW. Tel: 01222 231 021

Angela Kelsall Occupational Therapist, Resettlement Team, Ely Hospital,
Cowbridge Road West, Ely, Cardiff CF5 5XE. Tel: 01222 562 323

Clare Nissel Birchfield, Hudnalls Loop Road, St Briavels Common, Glos. GL15 6SG.
Tel: 01594 530 163

Lisa Seymour Ely Hospital, Cowbridge Road West, Ely, Cardiff CF5 5XE.
Tel: 01222 562 323

Finance

Mark Douglas Milbury Care Services, Garrick House, 2 Queen Street, Lichfield, Staffs
WS13 6QD. Tel: 01543 415 106 (formerly Cambridge Social Services)

Gary Nield National Development Team, St Peter's Court, 8 Trumpet Street,
Manchester M1 5LW. Tel: 0161 228 7055

Simon Whitehead Deputy Director, National Development Team, St Peter's Court,
8 Trumpet Street, Manchester M1 5LW. Tel: 0161 228 7055

Staff development

Barbara McIntosh   Project Manager, Changing Days, King's Fund, 11–13 Cavendish Square, London W1M 0AN. Tel: 0171 307 2647

Jim Thomas   Professional Development Centre, Foster Road, Trumpington, Cambridge. Tel: 01223 846 018

Transport

Nick Tyler   Centre for Transport Studies, University College London, Gower Street, London WC1E 6BT. Tel: 0171 391 1562

User involvement

Andrea Whittaker   Project Officer, King's Fund, 11–13 Cavendish Square, London W1M 0AN. Tel: 0171 307 2646

Easy-to-read summary

Introduction

This book has been put together in a way we hope will help anyone who wants to know what it says.

We hope that

- people with learning difficulties

- parents/families

- staff

- managers

will all be able to read it and find new ideas and good ways of working.

We hope the pictures and symbols will be helpful. Most are quite straightforward, but the ones below might need some explanation.

help/support

needs

services

strengths

together

work/job

Our thanks particularly for comments on this part of the book to Hereford Changing Days User Group.

Pictures and symbols taken from: *A Guide to Using Symbols*, Phoenix NHS Trust; *Rebus Glossary; Picture Communication Symbols*, Mayer-Johnson, People First publications, The Drawings Pack (NACVS, Sheffield).

Chapter 1

The most important things to do

This chapter is about the most important things we need to do to make good things happen in the lives of people with learning difficulties. These important things include:

- persuading managers and other top people that it must be done!

- making sure that the changes are what people with learning difficulties want

- organising services and the money that pays for them in a way that helps staff support people properly

- making sure that each person with learning difficulties has the chance to speak up for themselves and say what they want

3

- supporting people a lot more to be involved in their local communities

- having a plan to make all this happen.

Start to make changes now!

Some people say things are okay and don't have to be changed. Other people want to change things but think it is too difficult to give it a go. A lot of people find change frightening and threatening. So people who are really keen to start making changes – parents, staff and people with learning difficulties – need to work together and show they are determined to make things better.

a voice for people with learning difficulties

People with learning difficulties have a big part to play. Many who are going to day centres are unhappy with the services they are getting at the moment. The recent People First National Conference in Edinburgh passed a motion: '**day centres should not waste people's time or people's lives**'. Parents of children leaving school want their sons and daughters to go to college and have jobs.

Listen to what people want

Changes in services must be based on what men and women with learning difficulties say they want to do in their lives. People who can't speak for themselves must have someone who knows them very well to speak for them.

In Essex, 750 people with learning difficulties talked about how they would like their lives to be. They put the information into a report and presented it to the Social Services Committee. This helped social services set out a plan for services that was truly based on the views and wishes of the people who used them.

Help services to change and grow

Services often have too many rules. This can make it difficult for staff to help people in the way they would like. So this can mean that people with learning difficulties have less choice, are not allowed to take risks, or make changes in their lives from time to time. It helps if everyone working in services can keep learning, growing and developing and not get stuck in a rut!

Planning for each person's needs – person-centred planning

Every man and woman with learning difficulties should have a personal plan for their life. This should say:

- what is good about their life now

- what needs to change

- their hopes and dreams for the future

- what help and support they need to make their dreams come true.

Being included in the community

Many women and men with learning difficulties are now out and about in the community, using cafés, shops, restaurants, colleges and leisure centres. But often this still only happens in large groups, in separate places, special classes at college, special times at swimming pools, etc.

We still have to work hard to support people to be a part of the community like anyone else. This means, for example:

- not only going to watch the football match but perhaps being a member of the supporters' club and helping to run it

6

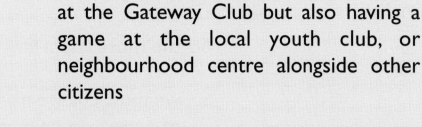

- not only playing snooker or table tennis at the Gateway Club but also having a game at the local youth club, or neighbourhood centre alongside other citizens

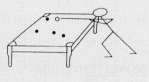

- not only going to a rock concert with a member of staff but with a friend who shares the same interest.

One way of helping people to be an active part of their community is to work with one person at a time.

It is also important to help the community to welcome people with disabilities and let them join in more with everyone else in the community. Services need to work with housing, employment, education, leisure and other organisations to help them make this happen.

They must help these organisations to understand that people with learning difficulties have the same rights as anyone else.

Moving from services to support for individual people

So the most important messages are:

- we must change from just helping groups of people to helping *each person* live the way they want with the support they need

- we must start by asking each man and woman with learning difficulties what they want in their future. Then give the support that each person needs.

Read more
You can read more about the important things to do on pages 1–9.

Chapter 2

Getting started

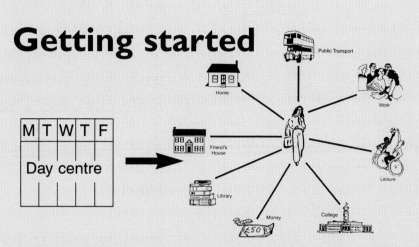

Many services are changing the way they work. They are moving away from big, separate day centres to supporting people to spend their days, evenings and weekends in the same places in the community that everyone else uses. How are services making these changes? They are doing it by:

- listening to what people with learning difficulties say they want in their lives

- listening to parents and staff say what changes they would like to see

- getting a group of people together to lead the changes

- making sure there are strong leaders to support people

9

- getting top people to believe in these changes and give their support

- making sure that each person with learning difficulties has a personal plan

- using these personal plans to build better services

- training staff to have new skills

- employing staff to work when people with learning difficulties need them – in the evenings and weekends as well as the day time

- getting jobs for people

- using money in different ways.

Hackney has made big changes to their services – read about it on page 21.

Sunderland has made big changes to their service – read about it on pages 22–23.

Cheshire County Council has made it possible for a lot of people to get jobs – read about it on page 24.

> **Read more**
> You can read more about getting started on pages 11–24.

Chapter 3

Staying on track

This means sticking with it, even when it gets very difficult!

Sometimes it is easy and exciting to make changes and see good things happening in people's lives. At other times, it is very difficult, people get upset and want to give up.

What helps?

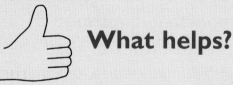

- Hold meetings to see how people are getting on and to support and encourage each other

- Celebrate success – tell people when they do something good and when good things happen

- Make special efforts to work with people who don't want change

- If you get stuck, try getting help and support from someone outside your local service

When managers and staff are trying to make big changes in services, it can be particularly difficult for those who are taking a lead. They need to make sure they get personal support for themselves.

It is important to work out a way of checking that the new service is doing what it set out to do. Managers and staff need to keep in touch with what is happening in the lives of people who use the service.

A good way of doing this is being developed by the Quality Is Our Business Too project. It worked with people with learning difficulties to choose ten important questions to ask people about their lives. You can read these questions on page 27.

Read more
You can read more about staying on track on pages 25–28.

Chapter 4

Strategic planning and commissioning

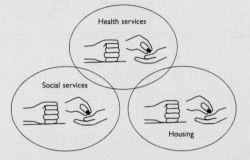

This chapter is particularly about commissioning services. People who commission services (commissioners) are sometimes called purchasers or buyers of services. But commissioners are more than that. They:

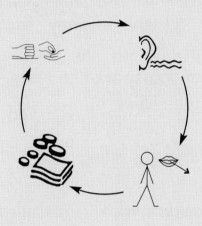

- find out how people with learning difficulties want to live their lives

- find out what help they need to do this

- use money and good ways of working to make sure people get the support they need

- keep in touch with people to make sure that is still what they want.

13

For commissioners to do their job well they need to:

- believe in the right of people with learning difficulties to have the same choices and opportunities as other citizens

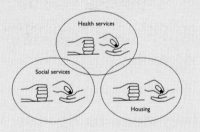

- have a planning system based on the needs of each individual

- use money in different ways according to what different people want. For example, instead of putting all the money for transport into contracts for big buses, use it for a variety of transport like taxis, cars which take wheelchairs, mini-buses, travel training, helping people use public transport or ride a bicycle safely

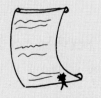

- work closely together with all their colleagues from different services

- make sure that planning is about a person's whole life – where they live, what they do during the day, getting a job, having a social life and friends

- write contracts which can change if someone's needs change

- make sure that the people who provide services – e.g. managers and staff in people's homes, staff who support people at work or college – understand very clearly how they should help men and women with learning difficulties.

It is important that commissioners keep in touch with people with learning difficulties who use the service. They can do this by:

- getting to know at least one person with learning difficulties very well

- taking part in service reviews that involve spending time with people

- setting up a way of getting regular comments and feedback from people who are using the service.

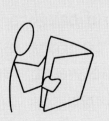

Read more
You can read more about strategic planning and commissioning on page 29–37.

15

Chapter 5

Getting a life, not a building

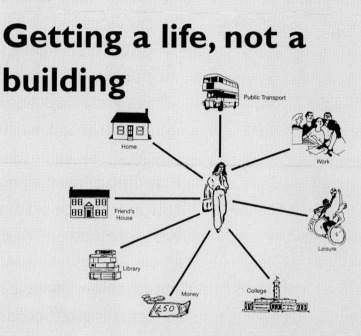

Many men and women with learning difficulties don't go to a day centre any more or perhaps go for just one or two days a week. This is because they have a job or go to college or do voluntary work or other activities during the day. This chapter is about how to support people to have interesting days without going to a day centre.

Using buildings differently

We cannot stop using big day centres overnight. Day centres are important places for people to meet their friends. Parents know that their sons and daughters are safe there. But it is difficult to make big changes for a lot of people while we still use all our traditional special buildings.

One way to start to make changes is to look at how we are using our buildings. Could they be used differently? Does your local area have a community centre? Could your day centre become a community centre for local people as well as people with learning difficulties?

Working without a day centre base

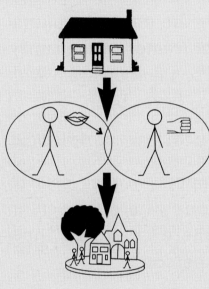

More people with learning difficulties are now being supported entirely in the community. The only special place is a small office for staff. Staff meet people at their homes and then go off together to do whatever is planned for that day.

It takes a lot of good planning, enthusiasm and commitment from everyone involved to make sure this type of support works well.

What helps?

- Staff who can work on their own, are good at meeting people, who know their own community

- A manager who trusts staff to take responsibility, manage their own time and get on with the job on their own

Linking with family and carers

Working in this way, staff get to know the person's family better. They see the family more often because they meet the person at their home rather than only seeing them at the day centre. This often means that staff can help people take part in more family activities.

They can get to know the person's cultural background. They meet friends of the family. They can help the person link up again with family members who have been out of touch.

It also means the support worker gets to know the neighbourhood where the person lives and where there may be new opportunities for the person.

Making it work for people with complex needs

Some of these community-based services support people with complex needs — women and men who need a great deal of support in their lives. Sometimes these are people who don't like going to the day centre because there are too many people or they find it noisy.

Often they are people who had so many problems they were not getting any service at all. It might be someone who is too afraid even to leave his/her own home. All these people are being helped by this kind of service.

The stories about Kevin and Ellen on pages 43 and 49 are good examples of how people's lives have changed.

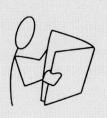

Read more
You can read more about non-buildings based services on pages 39–50.

Chapter 6

Getting involved in your local community

Every person with learning difficulties, no matter how severe their disabilities, should have the chance to live in the community and take part in local activities. Services should always work to make this happen.

Many people with learning difficulties are now getting out and about to a wide range of places in the community – leisure centres, colleges, pubs, shops, theatres and restaurants. But many people still go out in big groups and join in activities in the community only at special times – for example, they go swimming only at special sessions for disabled people, or attend special classes at college which are only for disabled people.

We need to do much more to help people also have the chance to go out with just one or two friends – for example, to see a film, to go to a concert or to join a photography club together.

We need to do much more to help people do things in the community alongside other citizens.

Friendships and relationships

Friendships are very important to all of us. When a day centre is closing, people who go to the centre often ask:

'How will I keep in touch with my friends?'
'How can I make new friends?'

Services must make sure that people can keep in touch with their friends and help them make new friends. In the past, services have not been good at doing this. They need to realise how important it is. They need to make sure staff understand it is an important part of their job.

Helping people make friends

Helping someone make new friends is not always easy. Many men and women with learning difficulties are separated from their families. They have not had opportunities to learn how to make friends. They may have lived with the same group of people for many years. The only people they know are staff. Staff are often so busy looking after people that they don't have time to help them make new friends.

What helps?

Ask the person with learning difficulties what she/he would like to do. Then find somebody who wants to do the same thing so that they could do it together. For example, going for walks, joining a steel band, making pottery. Many services have set up schemes to help this happen. They are sometimes called leisure partnerships or befriending schemes.

TalkAbout

Friends

The Hereford Changing Days group has written a book about making friends. It is entitled *TalkAbout Friends* and has pictures as well as words.

For more information contact: Changing Days User Group, Hereford Citizen Advocacy, 25 Castle Street, Hereford HR1 2NW. Tel: 01432 263757.

Circles of support

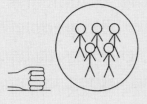

Every man and woman with learning difficulties should have at least one friend – one person in their lives who cares about them and wants to be with them. But most of us have a number of friends – some close friends and some friends we don't see so often. This should happen for people with learning difficulties too.

A good way to make this happen is to ask a few people to get together to help a particular person. This is called a 'circle of friends' or a 'circle of support'. The person with learning difficulties should choose who they want in their circle. It might just start with two people. Those two people also have friends who might like to join the circle. So, over time, the person with learning difficulties has a number of friends who they can see socially and call on for help if necessary.

A different job for staff

Staff need to work differently to make these things happen. It must become one of the most important parts of their work. They need to think of ways that will help men and women with learning difficulties meet more people and make more friends.

This is more than just finding a person 'something to do' in the community. It is about taking the time to help people make friends to know their neighbours, to become members of leisure and other community organisations, to help others as volunteers.

Staff will need to:

- be willing to speak up for people – to challenge prejudices

- be enthusiastic – want to make things happen for people

- be creative – able to think of new ways of doing things, find new opportunities

- be patient – it can take a long time – but stick to it!

Taking risks

Many parents, staff and carers worry about people taking more risks when they are out and about in the community. They worry about people having accidents, or meeting the wrong sort of people, or not knowing how to live safely away from the security of the day centre or hospital.

Some people with learning difficulties already know how to look after themselves very well. Others will learn quickly. Others will always need someone with them to make sure they are safe.

But whatever help people need, it should not stop them from trying out new things and taking part in activities they enjoy in the community.

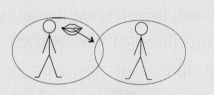

It is good that already so many more men and women with learning difficulties are out and about doing interesting things in the community. But we need to do much more to help people take part in their local community – just like other citizens do.

Read more
You can read more about creating inclusive communities on pages 51–65.

Chapter 7

Planning for individuals

 Each man and woman with learning difficulties should have their own plan of what they want their life to be like. This chapter is about how to draw up a lifeplan. The plan should set out:

- the person's hopes and dreams

- what they want to do in their lives

- the support they need to do it.

There are a number of different words used to describe people's plans:

> Lifeplan
> Assessment
> Profile
> IPP
> Community care plan.

There are a number of different ways of describing how to draw up these lifeplans:

> Whole life planning
> Personal futures planning
> Essential lifestyle planning
> PATH (Planning Alternative Tomorrows with Hope).

There is an example of a lifeplan and profile form in Appendix 7, on pages 196–204.

Each person should have a copy of their own lifeplan. The plan should be easy for the person to understand, use and share with other people as necessary.

Ways of doing this are:

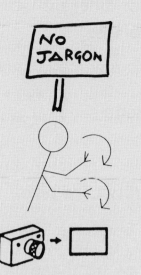

- use words the person understands

- use signs and symbols

- include photographs and drawings

- use videos and computers.

The lifeplan should look at the whole of a person's life and include:

- where they live

M | T | W | Th | F | S | S

- what they do in the day time, evenings and weekends

- what should be done to help them make friends?

- how to help them become members of local organisations and take part in their local community.

Making the lifeplan

Everyone who knows the person well – family, friends, staff, advocates and support workers – should be involved. The person should choose who they want to help them make their lifeplan.

It is important to record small details about the person, particularly if it is someone who can't easily say what he/she wants. 'Getting up' and 'going to bed' routines are important, but also smaller details like:

'Does he like to face towards light or away from it?'; 'Does she like to be fed a mouthful of meat before the vegetables – or vice-versa – or both together?' What sign does he use to say 'yes'? How do we know she is saying 'no'?

Make a life history book, including as much detail as possible about the person's past. This is very important in helping to understand what has happened to a person through their life. It can also tell us about interests or skills the person used to have which everyone has forgotten about.

For example:

A lady who lived at home until she was an adult was used to doing cooking, ironing and washing. She was put into an institution when her mother died and lost all these skills. When she moved out again into a house in the community, staff were surprised that she could do all these things.

The lifeplan should be the first step in developing a person's community care assessment. Information in the community care assessment is used by managers to decide what services a person needs. The people who do the community care assessment – the care managers – should know the person with learning difficulties very well, to make sure the person gets what they want and need.

Read more
You can read more about planning for individuals on pages 67–73.

Chapter 8

Keeping users central – the collective voice

Services must work in partnership with men and women with learning difficulties.

Everyone – from top to bottom of an organisation – must believe in working with users, understand why it is important and work to make it happen.

Money and staff for user involvement should be part of the main budget of the service, not just given when there is some 'spare money' or rely on staff to support user groups in their own time.

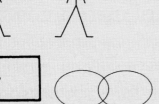

There should be opportunities for staff and users to train together.

A service that really wants to involve users will have:

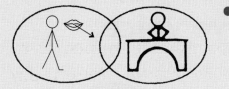

- senior managers and other 'top people' regularly meeting with men and women with learning difficulties:

    - planners and policy-makers attending user meetings

    - users attending council meetings

    - managers meeting with user representatives regularly

- users on committees and sub-groups with appropriate support

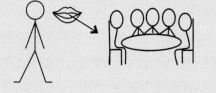

- parallel user groups with negotiating power and a clear process for joint working with staff/professional groups

- users actively involved in monitoring and evaluation

- user involvement written into contracts with providers.

To make sure individual users are involved the service will have:

- an individual lifeplan for each person and use the lifeplans to develop services

- a well-used complaints procedure

- users choosing their own support workers

- active user groups which have power to change things in residential homes, day centres and clubs

- user groups for people from minority ethnic groups

- staff specially appointed to promote user involvement

- easy-to-understand information about services in different languages and using signs and symbols, photographs, tapes, video and computers.

How users were involved in Changing Days

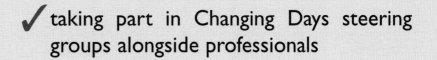

Three Changing Days user groups were set up – in Cambridge, Hackney and Hereford. These groups worked alongside the professional Changing Days groups.

Some of the good things the groups did:

✓ taking part in Changing Days steering groups alongside professionals

✓ speaking to social services committee members about their ideas for future day services

✓ visiting different parts of their own and other people's services

✓ making videos of their lives and services

✓ searching out new opportunities locally – places to go, things to do

✓ taking photographs to help people identify new staff and their new roles in services

✓ creating a booklet on things to do in the community which cost little or nothing

✓ writing a booklet on helping people make friends

✓ organising an activity day at the centres and inviting people from the community.

What helped?

The things that helped these groups grow strong were:

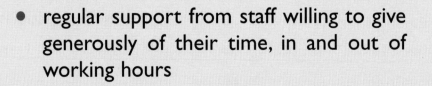

- regular support from staff willing to give generously of their time, in and out of working hours

- strong support from management – in writing and with money

- easy-to-read papers using everyday language and pictures

- managers keeping in regular contact with users

- professionals being willing to change the way they run meetings, the times and the places to fit in with users' needs.

Cambridge user group

CHANGING DAYS
IN
CAMBRIDGESHIRE

This is what members of the Cambridge group thought was good about being involved in Changing Days.

'Being able to meet new people and make new friends.'

'We have spent time out of the centre.'

'We have worked well in groups. It has been somewhere to talk about problems and worries.'

'We have worked with the steering group.'

'We have talked to managers about what we want.'

'We have invited guest speakers to talk to us.'

'We have had free lunches and drinks at meetings!'

Hereford user group

This is what members of the Hereford group said was good about being involved in Changing Days.

'Looking at what we like and do not like about our lives and the services we use.'

'Finding out about what others think and feel about things.'

'We want the user group to keep meeting and to grow.'

'We want to find out the views of service users and take them back to management and social services.'

'We want to go to centres and tell users what is possible and help them to stand up for themselves.'

Involving people with complex needs

Services should also listen to people who need a great deal of help, day to day in their lives. These people may need extra help to speak up. In Hackney, one young man was a member of the Changing Days user group right from the beginning. Although he could not speak, he could show how he felt about what was going on and helped the group remember the needs of people who have greater disabilities than themselves.

Some services now work together with the people with learning difficulties who use their services. A lot of work still needs to be done to make sure this happens in all services.

Read more
You can read more about involving users on pages 75–81.

37

Chapter 9

Involving parents and families

It is very important to work with parents.

 Parents want to talk about and be asked about changes in services.

 Many parents worry about big changes like closing a day centre. They are afraid that services are being cut and their sons and daughters will not receive the support they need.

 Parents want a reliable service. They want things to work properly. When their son or daughter has been attending a day centre five days a week, parents can be afraid of what he or she will be doing out and about in the community at different places, at different times, and on different days. Parents need to be sure that staff know where people are and what they are doing.

They want to be sure that their son or daughter is safe and not being put at risk.

Often parents who, at first, are angry and very much against any changes end up saying it is a good idea because they see how much better it is for their son or daughter.

Communication – talking together

Communication is very important to parents.

They say:

'Consult us right from the start'
'Listen to us'
'Be honest'
'Communicate regularly with us'

Ways of parents and staff working together

- Meetings – one-to-one (parent and staff member), small meetings (like workshops), larger meetings (like conferences), social events (when people can talk about other things besides services)

- Arrange visits for parents to go and see different services in other parts of the country.

- Give parents jobs to do – for example, in one new service, a parent whose everyday job was in transport chaired the sub-group looking at different kinds of transport

Many parents are looking for and welcome changes for their sons and daughters. But they also want to make sure that the new service will work for them too as well as their sons and daughters.

Read more
You can read more about involving parents and families on pages 83–90.

Chapter 10

Transition – moving towards adulthood

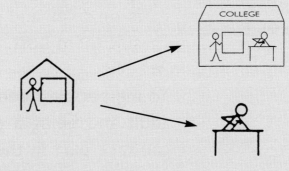

Transition means:

• getting ready to leave school

• thinking about what you want to do when you leave school – e.g. go to college, get a job

• planning how to make this happen.

It is a time when many important decisions about the future are made. To help make these decisions, young people with learning difficulties need to:

• talk to family, friends and staff about things they enjoy doing and would like to try

- talk to family and friends about college and work to get to know what it is like to be a student or an employee

- visit workplaces and colleges to see what is on offer and what sort of place would suit them best.

Young people need to learn about being an adult and being a good citizen so that they can take part in the life of their community.

The importance of information

Families need to be able to find information when they need it. The information must be correct and easy to understand.

The information should be about things like:

- a statement of rights

- a description of services available

- details of benefits and financial help

- where to go to talk to other people about transition

- how to make comments, suggestions or complaints.

Listen to people with learning difficulties

Sometimes young people with learning difficulties are not listened to properly. It's as if adults think they are still small children who don't have opinions of their own.

But when a young person is growing up, it is very important they are listened to by their parents, friends and staff. If they are treated with dignity and respect, they feel good about themselves and can look forward to the future with confidence.

Sometimes there can be problems when helping someone plan for their adult life:

the young person with learning difficulties wants one thing

the parents want something else

parents have strong ideas about what their son or daughter needs

staff have equally strong, but perhaps different ideas about what the young person needs

The young person is caught in the middle!

43

When planning for the future, young men and women with learning difficulties, their parents and families and staff must talk together about what they want and listen to each other.

You can read Beth and Michael's stories on page 92 and Aisha's story on page 96.

How can managers help?

- Involve young people with learning difficulties in all decisions about their life

- Appoint an advocate to help people who can't express their own views

- Parents, relatives and carers should be invited to attend transition planning meetings

- The meetings should be held at times and in places that are convenient to families

Read more
You can read more about transition on pages 91–99.

Chapter 11

Supported employment

 Having a job is very important to many men and women with learning difficulties.

 Even people with very severe learning difficulties can get jobs, provided they are given the right training and support.

In recent years, we have learnt a lot about how to help people:

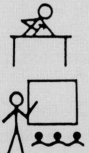 • get a job

• learn how to do the job

• keep on enjoying the job and doing it well.

Supported employment is a good way to help people get jobs because:

It is person-centred

It finds out what the person's interests are. It then finds the right job for the person, in the right organisation, in the right work surroundings

People get real jobs

They are jobs that employers need to pay somebody to do. The worker must do the job to the standard the employer needs. So the worker is helping to make the business a success

It is an ordinary working life

On-the-job training is very important. The person learns the skills necessary for that job

It helps the person learn to take risks

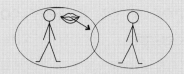 It provides opportunities for people with disabilities to spend time with non-disabled workmates

 It increases the amount of money people have to spend

How supported employment can improve services

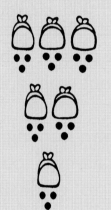 Although supported employment can cost a lot at the beginning, after a few years it costs less because:

- as workers need less support, less money is spent in paying staff to support them

- as workers need less support, staff can work with more people in the same amount of time.

 As more people get jobs and move out of day centres, fewer people go to the day centre. This gives day centre staff more time to work with people who don't wish to – or cannot – get a job.

Services can get extra money for supported employment. For example, from the European Social Fund, the Access to Work Scheme and Training and Enterprise Council funding.

Through a job people can make new friends and get involved in new leisure and recreation activities.

Problems in providing more supported employment

A number of things stop services being able to get jobs for more people. Sometimes it is because employment agencies aren't working well, but more often it is because of government policies about work and benefits.

Too often, the person with learning difficulties has to choose between having a job or having benefits. It is difficult to gradually reduce benefits as a person earns more in wages.

If a person loses his/her job, it can take a long time to get back on benefits.

The system for employing people does not allow for the fact that some disabled people can work well at some times but may be too ill at other times.

Sometimes there are problems because services don't understand what employers want. Services may think employers should give a person a job out of pity or charity. But employers need people who can do jobs well and help to run their businesses successfully.

What helps?

We need to:

- make sure that services and employers work together and learn to understand each other

- change the way money is used to provide supported employment

- change the way benefits are organised so that disabled people can more easily take up job opportunities.

Read more
You can read more about supported employment on pages 101–111.

49

Chapter 12

Access to continuing education

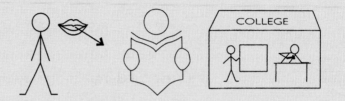

Many people with learning difficulties now go to college. Colleges are very important for helping people learn skills to get a job, make new friends and join in more leisure activities.

But we need to:

- help more people do real courses with a qualification – for example, NVQs

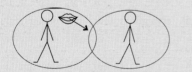

- make sure they go to classes alongside other students in the college – rather than attend special classes

- support them in a way which makes it possible for them to make new friends

- increase the number of minority ethnic students with learning difficulties who are going to college.

Elizabeth, Stan and Renu are three college students. Their stories are on page 114.

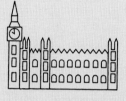

Recent government documents have changed the way education authorities work. These documents also say what should be done to make sure that all people with disabilities have the chance to go to college.

For example, the Further and Higher Education Act 1992 made colleges independent from local authorities. It also set out what courses colleges could teach.

The Further Education Funding Council was set up to make sure colleges do what the law says.

Some of these changes were good for people with learning difficulties. For example, more courses have to be about learning skills to get a job. More courses have to be planned so that people get a certificate at the end – for example, NVQ courses.

But some changes have not been good. For example, there are less courses just for fun – things like music, art and self-advocacy groups. This means there are often fewer classes that people with severe or profound learning difficulties can go to and enjoy.

One of the problems is that if colleges don't teach the subjects that the Further Education Council says they should teach, they don't get their funding. So some courses which people with learning difficulties particularly like are the ones that have been cut.

The Tomlinson Committee

This committee wrote an important report about what should be done for education for adults with learning difficulties. They asked colleges, local education authorities and other people what they thought about what the report said. Everyone supported the report. So in 1997/98, one million pounds (£1,000,000) is being used to train staff and produce training materials to help colleges include more people with disabilities.

Funding further education

There are a number of different ways of getting more money for education:

Further Education Funding Council
Local education authorities
European Social Fund
Health authorities and social services
Training and enterprise councils
Voluntary organisations
Joint funding.

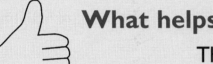

What helps?

There is a good action checklist on page 121 for staff and others wanting to help adults with learning difficulties go to college. Some of the things it suggests are:

- Support people to be involved in college committees and training staff

- Make sure there are taster sessions so that students can try out different classes before making a choice.

- Find the right class for each person, not just people to fill 'a class'

- Let the student choose something he/she is interested in and wants to learn

- Ask for easy-to-understand information. Many colleges still do not have details of their courses in large print, easy words and pictures or photos. If a college hasn't done this, offer to do it together and involve people with learning difficulties

- Ask for self-advocacy courses to be put on.

- Make sure that support workers know how to support students in class properly

- Offer to help education staff with training

Read more
You can read more about further education on pages 113–122.

Chapter 13

Making it happen for people with complex disabilities

Every person with learning difficulties – even people with complex needs or multiple disabilities – should live in the community like everyone else.

By people with complex needs we mean people who can't speak, walk or do anything for themselves.

They can also be people who:

- get angry a lot

- injure themselves

- sometimes attack other people.

The starting point for helping people with complex needs is the same as for anybody with disabilities:

- start with the hopes and dreams of the person

- look at what they can do rather than what they can't do

- give top priority to helping people communicate – to get over to other people how they feel, what they like and don't like, and what they want to do

- support each person to have a say in their choice of lifestyle.

For some men and women with complex needs, these things are happening and their lives have improved a lot. But there are many others who have not yet had these opportunities.

Helping a person with complex needs to live like everyone else in the community is not always easy and takes a lot of time. But more and more success stories are proving that it can be done.

Communication

Many people with severe learning difficulties don't speak or use signs and may even find pictures and photographs difficult. They rely on others to say how they feel and what they want to say. How can we help these people?

Other people with learning difficulties can help. For example, people who go to day centres often get to know people who are in the special care unit very well.

Managers must give staff enough time to get to know individual people very well.

Symbols and signing should be used more.

Make sure that people have sight and hearing tests in case this is what is making communication difficult.

Carly is a young lady who lives in Belfast. She is using video and a computer to help her communicate. Her story is on page 126.

Challenging behaviour

People who have a reputation for hurting themselves or others are often said to be 'not ready' to go into the community. But this is often because services are thinking only about what the person can't do, instead of what he/she can do.

If we get to know a person really well, we can learn how to help them. This may take a very long time but in the end the person's life can change for the better. Read the story about John on page 129.

People with challenging behaviour often don't see their family and have no friends. So it is very important to get people in their lives who care about them. Sometimes it can be someone they knew in the past. Or it might be long-lost members of their family, or staff from an institution where they used to live.

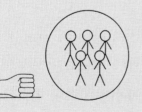

Brian was unhappy living in London and had no family to help him. He had one friend who introduced him to more people, and his circle of friends helped him move to a new home. Read his story on page 130.

Read more
You can read more about people with complex needs on pages 123–133.

Chapter 14

Keeping fit and healthy

People with learning difficulties should be able to get the same good quality health care as everyone else in the community. This means:

- going to a GP who knows the person well and is helpful

- taking part in health screening programmes (e.g. blood tests, allergies, tests for cancer)

- learning about healthy lifestyles (e.g. diet, exercise, sexual health).

People with learning difficulties often don't get good health care. For example:

- some doctors and other health care staff don't understand what their special needs might be

- they don't get so many health checks, such as immunisation, blood pressure checks, sight & hearing tests

- they sometimes find it harder to say how they feel or what's wrong with them

- people who have lived in long-stay hospitals often don't have good medical records. Important information about things like childhood diseases, seizures and drugs is often missing.

What helps?

Each person's individual profile or lifeplan should include a section on health care needs – the support he/she needs in order to keep healthy and fit.

People who find it difficult to say how they feel – to let others know when they feel sick – should have help with communication. Staff need to watch out for signs of pain or distress and keep a note of these to help others who don't know the person so well.

Every person should have a yearly health check with their GP.

When people go to their GP, they should be able to go with someone they choose who knows them well.

The National Development Team has developed an easy-to-use personal health record for people with learning difficulties. It is entitled *Advocating for Health* and is available from Harlow Print Ltd, on 0191 455 4286.

The need for services to work together

Men and women with learning difficulties can get good health care only if doctors, physiotherapists, social workers and care managers work together to make this happen.

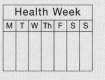

West Surrey Health Authority organised a week of health activities for people with learning difficulties and their families and carers. There were workshops and classes about personal safety, healthy eating, keep fit, sports and women's health. People with learning difficulties were involved in organising, advertising and taking part in the week.

You can read more about this Health Week on page 140.

The Healthy Way is a helpful booklet with tape and game expressly for people with learning difficulties. It is available from: Dept of Health, PO Box 410, Wetherby LS23 7LN.

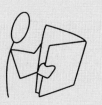

Read more
You can read more about health care in the community on pages 135–142.

61

Chapter 15

From hospital to community

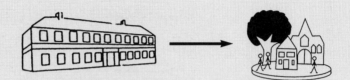

Planning how people moving out of hospital will spend their days, evenings and weekends should begin at the same time as planning where they will live.

The person's individual lifeplan should be used as a starting point.

Managers must make sure that money is in the budget specially to pay for daytime and weekend activities.

People who live in hospital are mainly looked after by health services. But when a hospital closes, other services like social services and voluntary organisations get involved.

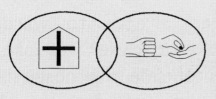

Staff from these services often work in different ways. They need to learn how to work together to make sure the people moving out of hospital will be happy in their new homes in the community.

In order to help overcome this problem, Ely Hospital employed two managers and two day services staff who usually worked in social services. These people had their office at the hospital so they could get to know residents and work closely with hospital staff.

Keeping person-centred

In order to make sure that each person living in Ely Hospital was treated as an individual, the following things were done:

• Planning circles were set up to help each resident have a say in their choice of lifestyle in the community.

Read about Mike Hooking's planning circle on page 149.

- Money was given directly to ward managers to make it easier to take people to places outside the hospital. Before this, staff had to fill in a lot of forms or go to the petty cash office before people could, for example, go out for a day trip at the weekend.

Recording past life history

Unfortunately, when people have lived in hospital for many years, information about their lives – their family backgrounds, people they have known – is often lost when they leave hospital. Sometimes this is because their records have been lost. Sometimes it is because staff in the hospital who have known them for many years don't have a chance to pass on information.

It is very important that as much information as possible is written down before people leave hospital. It is also important that photographs and other links with their past go with them.

Life outside hospital

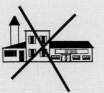

When people leave Ely Hospital, they are not going to day centres. Each person has a programme of activities which use ordinary places in the community.

In Cambridge, a number of young people who need a great deal of support in their lives and who used to live in Ida Darwin Hospital are now living in an ordinary house in the community. Each day they go out to different places in the community with staff who are specially employed to help them with their days, evenings and weekends.

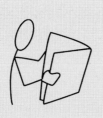

Read more
You can read more about moving from hospital to community on pages 143–152.

Chapter 16

Finance

New-style day services will mean that managers need to work out new ways of using money.

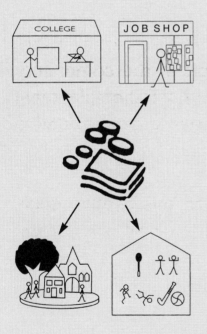

At present, a lot of the money for services is used up in buildings. But new services are much more about people than buildings. It is also about people going to a number of different places during the week instead of just one place – the day centre. This means that it is more complicated to run the service. So the way the money is used will be more complicated.

Also, money is coming from different places. Not just social services, but health, education, European Social Fund and many others. This also makes things more complicated.

There are no easy answers on how to organise the money better.

Some of the questions are:

When a person needs help to manage their money, who should take responsibility? Family, friends, advocates, health, social services, voluntary agency?

If someone wants to change their personal plan and do something different, how do we make sure they will be able to use their money to pay for the different activities?

We need money for making more opportunities for people in the community. We need money for supported employment services. We want people to be included in their local community.

The funding to make all this happen could come from many different places. How can we sort this out?

What will help?

Everyone believing that people come first and sticking to it!

All the different services working together to make the best use of their money and skills.

67

Helping men and women with learning difficulties get more money. This can be done by helping more people get jobs and by giving good advice about benefits.

Commissioners and providers need to have a plan to get the new service going and then work closely together to find the best ways of using money for the benefit of people who use the service.

Read the story of the Kingsthorpe Lighthouse on page 160. This describes a way of using money differently to help people have more opportunities.

Direct payments

Social services can now give money to disabled people to buy their own services and support. This money is called a 'direct payment'. Direct payments can give people more independence and choice about how to live their lives.

A few people with learning difficulties already get direct payments. Some people use the money to buy help they need to live in their own homes. Other people use it to help them get to work or go out in the evenings or weekends.

Turn to page 161 to read Gary Nield's story. He used his direct payment to employ someone to help him at home and during the day.

It's your right:

- to ask for information about direct payments

- to ask if you can have a direct payment

- to get help to use your direct payment.

You can get more information about direct payments from 'Plain Facts'. Ask for a copy of Issue 10, June 1997. Write to: Plain Facts, Norah Fry Research Centre, 3 Priory Road, Bristol BS8 1TX. Tel: 0117 9238137.

A useful book about money is: *It's My Money* by Catherine Bewley, a book and tape for people with learning difficulties. £3.00. From: VIA Publications, Oxford House, Derbyshire Street, London E2 6HG. Tel: 0171 729 5436.

Read more
You can read more about finance on pages 153–163.

69

Chapter 17

Staff development

Training is a very important part of making changes in services.

Staff, service users and carers should all be included in training.

Training can:

- change the way people think about their organisation and their work

- introduce new ideas

- help people develop new skills

- make it easier to change services.

There should be a training plan which says what training will be done and how it will be done.

What training needs to be done?

It is important to find out what skills people will need for the new service. Ask people what they think their training needs are.

It is important to organise training which people need – not just about things they know already!

Including service users and carers

It might be necessary to run training for service users or carers in the evenings or at weekends.

Send out letters to make sure that service users and carers know the training is available.

Service users and carers might find it helpful for trainers to visit them and explain what the training is and why it might be useful.

Different ways of training

Conferences are good for getting everyone together and collecting people's ideas. But many people find it hard to speak up in a large group.

Training which runs over several days is good for helping people work as a team and for learning new skills.

Workshops are also good for helping people learn new skills. They are usually for one or two days.

Was the training successful?

At the end of the training session, it is important to ask participants what they thought.

Good training can be a great help to staff, service users and carers and it does not have to cost a lot of money. But it does require support from all those who want to change services for the better.

Read more
You can read more about staff development on pages 165–173.

72

Chapter 18

Transport

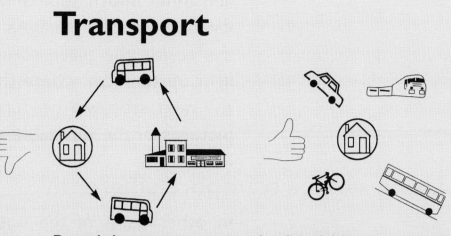

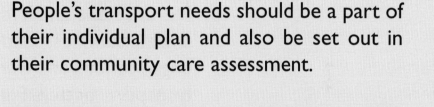

People's transport needs should be a part of their individual plan and also be set out in their community care assessment.

Every person with learning difficulties should have the opportunity to have good travel training.

Turn to page 180 for a list of things which should be included in travel training.

Public transport must be designed to make it easier for people with learning difficulties.

Mare Street

Nightingale Flats

The Hackney Plus Bus is a service which is something like an ordinary bus and something like a Dial-a-Ride service. All the information about the service is designed to make it easy to understand. Each bus stop along the route has a different symbol like those on the left.

These pictures are printed on timetables and other information and are inside the bus itself on a display panel. As the bus goes along the route, the place name and the picture light up to show where the bus is and what the next stop will be. Turn to page 181 for pictures of the timetable and the route.

Using service transport differently

In other parts of the country, for example Devon, Kent and West Norfolk, health and social services, education and voluntary organisations are working together to make transport better. For example, they share the use of the different vehicles they own. The buses travel to different places and at different times according to what disabled people need.

Buying your own transport

Many more people are now buying or leasing (hiring) their own vehicles – cars or vans – using mobility allowance and other personal savings. The vehicle may be used by one person or by two or three people in the same house, putting all their money together. At Ely Hospital a vehicle was bought for one ward using the money of the people living on that ward.

Read more
You can read more about transport on pages 175–182.

Chapter 1

The essential elements

In recent years – and particularly the last three years of the Changing Days project – we have learnt much about what is required to make positive change happen for individual people. The essential elements are listed in the box.

Key ingredients

- Creating a commitment to change with a sense of urgency
- Capturing people's vision of how life could be
- Creating a culture of change and development
- Person-centred planning
- Understanding inclusion
- Moving from services to support for individual people
- Making it happen: having a gameplan

There is much more about these elements later in the book, but it is important early on to recognise that if you really mean to improve opportunities for men and women with learning difficulties to develop and lead lives of their own choosing, there are some key ingredients without which you are bound to fail.

Creating a commitment to change with a sense of urgency

It seems obvious that you will not achieve change unless people see the need for it, but so many attempts to do better fail because people central to that change fail to see the need for it. *'If it's not broken, why try to fix it?'* is a sentiment often expressed by those in leadership positions, as well as parents and sometimes by staff in services. Even if the need for change is acknowledged, without a sense of urgency little or nothing will happen.

So where does commitment to change in day services come from? The following box shows some examples of actions that have led to change either directly or by skilful presentation.

Opportunities for change

- *Making it a human rights issue.* Although this should be central to the motivation for change – people being denied access to work, education, opportunities for friendship, choices in their daily lives – the urgency is not so pressing as the case for moving from hospital to community. However, constant talk about human values and the hypocrisy of agencies that espouse them but continue to run segregate, congregate day services can sometimes make more of an impact when it comes from influential people.

- *Creating a crisis out of demand.* Most existing day services are severely stretched for space, staffing capacity and increasing demand from people leaving school, coming out of hospital, growing older and not moving on. This can force senior managers and planners to think about what they provide and for whom.

- *Creating a crisis out of dependency.* Anecdotal evidence suggests there are many people with high levels of dependency in, or waiting to attend, day services. This has resource implications and leads us to ask who currently attends these centres, who needs to, and more fundamentally, are centres the right approach anyway?

- *Harnessing the forces for change – creating a critical mass.* Many people who use existing services are very dissatisfied with them. The recent People First national conference in Edinburgh passed a motion: *'Day centres should not waste people's time or people's lives'.* A growing number of parents – many of them young people – who have experienced better schooling for their sons and daughters, wish to avoid what they see as the 'dead end' of day centres. Their views and energy can lobby the appropriate agencies for change.

- *Opportunities arising from existing buildings/sites.* Many opportunities for change stem from problems with the buildings currently occupied by services. These are often inappropriate older-style commercial buildings on industrial estates which usually are in urgent need of repair or radical alterations; some of these sites have become valuable properties and could be sold for a good price. Situations such as these can be seized on to demand a review of current service provision and prompt a service redesign.

- *Saving money.* Where there is substantial investment in day services as with larger authorities, the possibility of even modest savings in the long term can persuade people that a fundamental review of existing provision is needed with all the opportunities this presents.

This is not an exhaustive list, but illustrates how changes have been sparked in some areas. The greater the range of arguments, the greater the sense of urgency that can be created. The other main cause of urgent action arises from personal injuries or abuse; while these are obviously unfortunate, clearly they are situations that can be exploited to review current practice.

Capturing people's vision of how life could be

If there is going to be change then it must be informed centrally by the needs and wishes of those people who use or want a service. Too often it is assumed that staff or parents 'know' what people want or they somehow glean the information from conversations or existing Individual Programme Planning (IPP) processes. To transcend the limitations of what currently exists, people need the opportunity to think imaginatively 'outside' and share their ideas and dreams about what might be possible.

In 1996 the National Development Team helped Essex Social Services Department undertake an extensive consultation exercise with service users across the county. A group of staff were trained as 'listeners' who then went out and met over 750 people with learning disabilities in a number of different places and situations, and talked with them about their vision of life as they would like it to be. These visions were collated and a group of service users were assisted to produce an accessible report for wide dissemination, and to make a powerful presentation to the social services committee. This process enabled the department to develop a model for services that was wholly informed by the opinions and wishes of the people who used them.

There are other ways of doing this, of course, but this method highlights the fact that it can be done on a large scale and also done in a way that will legitimise and maximise the thrust for change. Other techniques such as PATHs[1] can be adapted to working with groups of people on strategic visioning. Support or facilitation from outside the agency can be effective in making both the process and the outcome more credible.

Creating a culture of change and development

People are generally conservative by nature and find change unsettling or even frightening. In many ways our services are designed to protect people from uncertainty by having policies, procedures, rules, job descriptions, hierarchies of authority and accountability that concentrate on static systems rather than development. Paradoxically, we have created a system that may feel safe but which actively works against those very things necessary to make them more relevant to individuals – flexibility, risk-taking, choice, diversity and creativity.

The natural forces against change are inherent and strong. The only sure way to counter them is to create a culture that encourages change and development and also provides security through job satisfaction. Some of the key features of such a 'learning' culture or organisation are listed in the box.

A learning organisation

- A sustained commitment to the vision through strong leadership
- Living with and tolerating ambiguity
- A willingness to work across agency and service boundaries
- A project rather than a systems focus
- An emphasis on growth and choice instead of solutions
- A willingness to learn from mistakes and try again
- Staff who are valued and an investment made in their development
- Encouraging the asking of questions
- Accepting that the appropriate personal involvement in people's lives is support
- Being open to criticism
- Encouraging and supporting innovation and new ways to do things
- Seeing change as an opportunity rather than a threat
- Setting aside time for reflection and to learn new things
- Constantly asking 'how can we do better?'

These attributes cannot be acquired overnight and they all require strong and sustained leadership within the organisation if they are to be achieved.

Person-centred planning

The core truth is that if people are to be supported to live their own lives, then the starting point is a thorough process of person-centred planning. This seems to be increasingly recognised but the bad news is that while many now accept this, progress and its successful implementation seem woefully slow. Why?

There appear to be two main problems: the first is about definition of the term 'person-centred planning'; and the second is about understanding what happens to it when it is implemented widely after successful trials with just a few individuals.

Person-centred planning is called different things by different people to describe a variety of circumstances and different contexts – personal futures planning, essential lifestyle planning, circles of support, MAPs, and PATHs (see references). It is important to seek the common elements behind these different approaches and techniques.

Although person-centred planning can work dramatically for some people, it is dangerous to 'systematise' it and hope it will work for everyone. The history of Individual Programme

Person-centred planning

IS	is NOT
Empowering individuals to begin to take control over their own lives and make difficult choices between conflicting opportunities and challenges.	A system for collecting information about someone to enable others to make decisions, with or without their involvement.
Listening to people who are important in someone's life and helping them to explain their views and feelings and achieve their wishes.	A set of questions to or about someone on a form that will allow the questioner to know what that person wants or what is best for them.
Getting to know someone properly by spending time with them as an individual, not in some service giver/receiver relationship.	Another way to think of strategies to make people do something or behave somehow differently.
Working with people's capacities and achievements, and not their deficiencies.	A way to ration resources. It may need to stand alongside assessment and care management systems as it will not effectively replace them and keep to its purpose.
Personal commitment to someone often outside normal system or programme boundaries.	

Planning (IPP) demonstrates what happens when good processes get institutionalised. Some argue that person-centred planning cannot by its nature be central to system change; but this is to deny the reality that systems often stand in the way of people's dreams and aspirations.

Person-centred planning has to be at the heart of *both* empowering the individual *and* enabling the service system to adapt and change. But to do so, person-centred planning has to be used with what John O'Brien (quoting from a book by Ellen Langer in an unpublished paper) describes as 'mindfulness': 'an ideas utility lasts only as long as people apply it mindfully ... any tool's power can be diluted or even misdirected by its mindless use'. Mindfulness has three characteristics – the continuous creation of new categories, openness to new information and an implicit awareness of more than one perspective. If we forget why and how person-centred planning helped some people – the mindful way we directly engaged with somebody – its purpose will be lost and it will become another 'hula hoop in the museum of past fads'.

Understanding inclusion

If there were only two key elements in helping make people's vision a reality and one was person-centred planning, the other would be inclusion in the community. And if getting to grips with person-centred planning is difficult, then the idea of inclusive community is even more complex.

Inclusion is not just about 'being in' the community; more importantly it is about being able to participate actively in it. It is about creating opportunities for individuals to be included and also about how the community itself adapts to become more inclusive to disadvantaged people so that they turn into valued respected citizens. Indeed community membership is sometimes described as citizenship.

People with learning disabilities have been consistently excluded for many years – both by their communities and by the services that deliberately segregated them. Undoing this legacy is therefore at the heart of the matter. As services address the issue of becoming enablers and supporters rather than care providers, so the wider community is beginning to address the issue of acceptance and inclusion of people back into the mainstream of life – work, education, leisure, social networks, ordinary health care and so on.

We know a lot about moving people physically into the community; most now live in houses in local streets and towns, albeit residential care in many instances. Many use various community facilities, either through existing day services or by direct access; many use further education and other community-based leisure and recreational opportunities. Sadly, these activities are often still undertaken in large groups, and sometimes still in segregated settings – special classes, special times in swimming pools and the like. We have been less successful in actively engaging people in integrated activities and supporting them in their development of strong social networks of relatives, friends, neighbours, etc. Peter Bates has illustrated this graphically in an unpublished paper as the four components of community connection (see Appendix for complete chart).

Components of community connections

Going out – leaving the residential or day care building for any reason (e.g. to increase experiences, develop interests, topics of conversation)

Community amenities – places to shop, eat, drink, walk, look (e.g. to develop independence, reduce use of specialist services)

Integrated pursuits – joining a group of citizens without apparent disabilities to work, learn or enjoy leisure time

Social networks – relatives, friends, neighbours, colleagues who care (e.g. for companionship, practical help, emotional support, increase network of contacts)

Research confirms our suspicion that while existing services do well at supporting going out and are getting a lot better at community amenities, the opportunities for integrated pursuits are less, and the development of strong social networks few and far between. Social networks do not happen easily and are difficult to create; they only arise where people are supported into situations where opportunities for them to develop already exist, and where paid services are willing and able to hand over to ordinary people, sometimes referred to as 'fading'.

Working directly with individuals supporting community participation is one aspect. The other challenge is how to make a community more accessible and ultimately more inclusive. Indeed, can we 'make' a community inclusive?

There are clearly issues such as discrimination, changing attitudes and influencing the general public that are bigger than social services or related agencies can handle – although the way a service works, the messages it gives and the image it supports, all play their part in this wider social movement. More specifically, it is essential to influence generic services at the local level: to work with housing, employment, education, leisure and other services to help them recognise the need for accessibility, challenge their own discrimination, and create new opportunities for people. Men and women with learning difficulties have the same rights as everyone else to their services and resources.

There has been a growth in the development of specialist roles or projects and there are now even separate services engaged in community bridge-building. We have supported employment agencies whose job it is to work with employers and the employment service to create work opportunities for people generally and individually. Similar examples exist in further education and in leisure services. One of the lessons from this is that people directly supporting individuals cannot do all the community bridge-building; and in many respects the skills are different.

Moving from services to support for individual people

There is a growing conviction that simply moving from one service model to another only replicates many of the difficulties of the former. The question has now become:

'How can we turn a service that serves everyone alike into one that enables individual people to develop lives of their own choosing with the appropriate personal supports?'

So it is not about a clever piece of service design or re-design with definable inputs, clusters of need and blocks of service response. It is about a different starting point and finishing line:

No special buildings, no special places. This feels very difficult because it does not tell us how to replace the existing day service. The answer is, we do not replace it: we start to work differently with people as individuals until we have created a new style of personalised support. We may have to make changes to the service along the way: it may become economically impractical and have to be 'downsized' or moved. This might be the only way to release the resources. The vision will not be achieved by changing the service – it may be necessary to change the service in the process of delivering the vision.

Making it happen by developing a gameplan

Why does it feel so overwhelming? Because it is not a simple 'replace one thing with another' job; because it involves doing things we thought we were good at (like listening to people) differently; because it involves many new participants in areas with which services have had little experience; because it means replacing a single, identifiable, costed service for x people, with x different, diverse, difficult-to-cost arrangements.

It can be done on a small scale and there are many examples to prove it. There are many answers that show us how to make it happen for one or two people. But making it happen for many people seems much more complex. More time should be given to designing a process in which the overall vision is identified, and detailed work done on the steps needed to make progress with proper identification of the pitfalls and opportunities along the way. Designing the process must include all those people crucial to making it happen. This can be called the gameplan and there are a variety of tools and techniques available to help its development. It may be appropriate to bring in outside help.

Key steps in the change process

John Kotter, an American writer, has pointed out what inhibits effective change in person-centred services. This can be presented as eight key steps for making things happen:

- Establish a sense of urgency
- Create a guiding coalition – a group working as a team with the power to lead the change
- Develop a vision to help direct the change and a strategy for achieving it
- Communicate the change vision and strategy – getting broad ownership of the approach, and communicating regularly with all stakeholders
- Empower broad-based action – overcoming obstacles, changing systems and structures, encouraging innovation
- Achieve early results and successes so that people see change happen quickly with positive outcomes
- Consolidate gains and produce more wins – using increased credibility to change wider systems and structures, bringing in new leaders and developers
- Anchor new approaches in the culture – developing quality safeguards, reinforcing new skills and attitudes, ensuring leadership development and succession

Adapted from John Kotter, *Why Transformation Efforts Fail.* Harvard Business School, 1995.

Conclusion

After all the experience of change in services and in the lives of people with learning disabilities over the past thirty years, we should now know something about what works and what does not. This chapter has sought to articulate some of the key elements that seem the most important at the moment. There is growing belief that real progress is and will be made only if we take the person-centred route. We understand more and more about this, and should now be ready to make that final move beyond the provision of special services.

References

1. Pearpoint J, O'Brien J, Forest M. *PATH (Planning Alternative Tomorrows with Hope). A workbook for planning possible positive futures.* Toronto: Inclusion Press, 1993.

Chapter 2

Getting started

Many individuals and organisations are already considering change in their day services and the Department of Health has encouraged social services departments and others to think about new and different approaches. The will to change is there, confirmed by the rapid expansion of local projects that help people with learning difficulties get jobs.

But most of these schemes are small, one-off initiatives. It has been much harder for organisations to develop systematic and strategic approaches to changing day services across a whole locality. The vision certainly exists – in statements about individualised programmes, jobs, supported leisure activities and access to mainstream further education. But the mechanics of shifting from the current infrastructure based on large day centres to realising the vision are missing.
(Changing Days, 1996)

Across the UK there are increasing moves away from large segregated centres to supporting people in ordinary everyday settings. This wave of change has been influenced by:

- the expressed wishes of men and women with learning difficulties to be full participants in society and make choices about their preferred lifestyle
- the belief that the strengths and abilities of individuals are better used and developed in non-institutional and non-segregated settings
- pressure from staff, users, parents and managers to improve and provide inclusive services
- the relative success of supported employment, leisure and education as an alternative for everyone, including people with complex needs, in achieving the inclusion of people in the community
- collaborative working across key agencies, including health, voluntary and independent sectors
- government directives: 'local authorities should plan to shift away from services based on attendance at traditional adult training centres towards an approach to day services based on individual assessment and programmes ... the aim should be to move towards a personally planned programme of day activities, social, educational, vocational and leisure which makes use of ordinary community facilities wherever practicable.'[1]

Step-by-step from day centres to community

Raise awareness; what's good about the day service?
What needs to change?

Get agreement from senior managers, elected members, board members for changes.

Set up a 'change' group to steer the way forward.
Involve users, community members, employers, staff and carers.
Develop a communication strategy which keeps people
informed about and involved with changes.

Staff development to move to a person-centred service which supports
individuals to participate in ordinary activities in an inclusive community.
Undertake person-centred plans (PCPs).
Develop circles of support for each person.

Hold a stakeholders' conference to engage a wide group of people
in the change process and capture their ideas for the future.
Visit examples of innovation and good practice.

Use outcomes from person-centred plans and information from
stakeholders' conference to draft a framework for future services.
Create new job descriptions for staff.

Move resources (staffing and finance) to individual support for users (direct payments),
invest in supported employment, and community-based opportunities.

Get started on helping people (one-by-one) to participate in
new activities, jobs, education opportunities.
Ensure risk assessments are used to minimise problems.

Find new alliances for additional funding (e.g. TEC,
Welfare to Work programmes, corporate sponsorship).

Measure improvement in people's lives by looking at original PCPs.

Improve opportunities.

A plan for action

- Raise awareness about the problems of existing day services (while acknowledging and preparing for the criticism that change will bring)
- Create a culture of change which keeps people using services at the centre of the vision for the future
- Produce a strategy for the future service based on person-centred plans done with each service user
- Arrange for staff to be trained in person-centred planning
- Seek agreement from your social services committee to create a strategy for change and generate commitment from senior managers, carers and staff
- Set up a 'change' group which represents all interested groups and takes a lead on putting new opportunities in place
- Hold a stakeholders' conference to create enthusiasm, shape the vision of the future, encourage creativity and address fears and criticisms
- Engage a wide range of people in the change, including employers, voluntary organisations, adult community and further education colleges and leisure providers

A plan for action

Desire for change brings with it realisation of the need to plan and move forward simultaneously on a number of fronts, all of them equally important. Devising a plan of action which successfully balances all these priorities is the first challenge for everyone involved.

Creating a vision

Change cannot be imposed: it must be owned by everyone. The first step is to listen to what users, staff and carers say they feel works and doesn't work about existing services. Ask those who use the services and their carers what an ideal future would be like. Hearing the stories of people who have moved out of day centres into jobs and education is a powerful way to change hearts and minds. Parents and staff must be given opportunities to express their hopes and fears about change and the future. If people have real responsibility throughout the process of change they are more likely to be committed to it.

A change group

Achieving your vision for the future will be helped by setting up a change group. This should include users, carers, employers, staff and community groups. Users should be encouraged and supported to take part in this but may also like to have their own parallel group which feeds into the core group. (See Chapter 8 'User Involvement'.)

This change group can:

- do an audit of current services
- develop the strategy
- help analyse information received from person-centred plans
- lobby others to support the changes
- drive through the changes while supporting and re-energising one another.

The change group – and other people who use services, carers and staff – will be keen to learn about examples of change across the country. Arrange visits to innovative, successful examples of new services and share information with others. (See examples of good practice – Liverpool and Flintshire in *Changing Days*; and Hackney and Sunderland in this volume.)

Leadership

Major organisational change is almost impossible without positive leadership. That is, leadership not just at the top of the organisation, but throughout, including men and women who use the service, their parents and carers, front-line staff, employers in the community, and senior politicians and managers.

Leaders play a powerful role in initiating, emphasising, pursuing, supporting and sustaining change. A leader's role is to provide a structure through which staff energy may be channelled in working towards a common vision. The most effective leaders are risk takers who are passionate about improving the quality of people's lives while having a clear vision about how to do so. They instil in staff a sense of personal commitment while providing guidance and encouraging innovation.

Effective leaders

- Motivate people
- Establish a good organisational climate
- Create a range of networks to perpetuate change
- Achieve a powerful organisational philosophy
- Take decisions when there is uncertainty
- Cope with risk while recognising that even the best planning cannot identify all the problems that may arise
- Begin to make changes without everything being in place
- Cope with an incremental model of change and the difficulties this can bring
- Encourage innovation and seek alternative forms of funding
- Feel comfortable with a non-hierarchical approach where responsibility for change is devolved to a range of users, carers and staff.

Parents as partners

Include parents in the change group and make sure their views are taken on board and woven into your future vision of the service. Many will suspect change means cuts in services and getting started will mean acknowledging and responding to their anxiety and fear.

We continue to hear stories of parents feeling they are kept at arm's length and not fully involved in the planning process. Services need to tap into the leadership potential of parents and enable them to work alongside staff in seeing the changes through.

See Chapter 9 for detailed discussion on involving parents and what they want from services.

> ### Listening to stakeholders
>
> A successful stakeholders' conference will have the following elements:
>
> - a strong focus on the voice of people with learning difficulties
> - time spent hearing what people want to do with their days, evenings and weekends
> - plans under way to make this happen for individuals
> - everyone fully involved, knowing their views are listened to and valued
> - criticism and concern about change recognised and expressed
> - broad agreement reached on the principles and values of the future service
> - action agreed on the day and results beginning to be seen shortly afterwards.

A stakeholders' conference

Very early on in the process, you will need to bring all stakeholders together to obtain a collective view on how people see the future. As well as users, parents and other carers, and service people at all levels, participants should include local councillors and health authority members, local employers and people who can promote community participation.

Getting people on board

Alongside this will run preparation for obtaining the necessary political and resource approval of elected members and board members. The support of senior managers is essential in preparing elected and board members to accept change; they have an overview of resources and will need to agree any financial changes, and they are also linked to senior managers in other departments such as education, leisure and employment. We need them to help but they will do so only if you work to get them on board. Senior managers have to deal with the possible consequences if things go wrong. As one director of social services said: *'These changes scare me to death, but I'll back you.'* This type of support is essential.

Good collaboration with the independent sector and health and social services is also vital.

✓ Helping things move forward

♦ Meet people in person and talk to them about your ideas. In one instance when a new community-based service was being set up the person leading the change put a lot of effort into talking to local councillors and keeping them informed over time. When the service was finally introduced, the councillors felt a sense of ownership in the new venture and supported it enthusiastically

♦ People who have successfully introduced change often mention the need to become a 'super salesperson'. You may need all your powers of persuasion to ensure that key people are on board

♦ Base proposals for the future on hard facts and figures about unmet needs and the current design of the service. Use information from the person-centred plans, satisfaction surveys and finance data to compare your service with others around the country

♦ Invite stakeholders to visit services and show them the difficulties at first-hand. Let them listen to people with learning difficulties speaking about their hopes and wishes

♦ Highlight the possible consequences of standing still and increasing dissatisfaction

♦ Arrange to meet younger parents with school-age children. This group have higher expectations and a different vision of the future for their children

♦ Show that it can be done and point out where your local services are falling behind

♦ Ask for help and advice from local employers, community groups and civic leaders. Service clubs, such as Rotary, local volunteers centres, business development organisations, leisure services and community development organisations also have an important part to play

♦ Be honest about the possible difficulties. Show that you have thought about them and that you have contingency plans for addressing problems

♦ Search out possible allies

♦ Make sure you involve your chief executive. She or he will have a bird's-eye view of the situation and be a good ambassador once convinced that change is necessary

Gaining support from important stakeholders

Give thought to those stakeholders who are likely to support change and those who could hinder progress. Where people are potential allies, you need their help as soon as possible. If there are people likely to block change, you need to deal with this, too, as soon as you can. Although it is often tempting to delay talk about change (especially to those who might oppose it), it is better to start discussions as early as possible. People who have been involved in generating ideas are more likely to feel they 'own' them.

In one area, a group was set up to consult with parents and relatives of people moving out of a long-stay hospital. However, members of the group had in the past had some uncomfortable experiences with relatives and were wary of working with them. As a result, they spent a lot of time discussing tactics but never quite made the jump of working with them. The breakthrough came when the group decided to set up a small meeting with some of the relatives, a few of whom had positive experiences of community living for their family members. The meeting went well and led to a series of others which in turn drew in more people. Although not everyone was completely won over, the group still successfully set up effective working relationships and was able to involve relatives in their planning process.

Planning for individuals; person-centred planning

The first step towards your future service plan is to have a good individualised planning system with a clear statement of what each person with learning difficulties wishes to do and the skills they possess to achieve this. There are a number of different personal planning systems to choose from and these are discussed in more detail in Chapter 7. Recent developments in the use of computers and video material, such as multi-media profiling, provide valuable tools to assist with these plans and are particularly helpful with people who do not communicate verbally.

A circle of support

A network of friends and supporters, or a circle of support, is an important way of focusing on the individual concerned and achieving the goals set out in their plan. A circle of support may include one or two members of staff but the emphasis is on non-service people – friends, family, neighbours and acquaintances. The circle meets regularly to help the person build bridges to everyday community life such as finding a job or joining social groups. Circles also work to overcome a variety of barriers that service systems often create.[2]

In Cardiff, people who are preparing to move out of Ely Hospital take part in a planning circle. This involves all the key people in their life – paid staff, friends and relatives. The circle meets regularly and is very task-oriented, focusing on what that person wishes to do and ways to make it happen.

Planning for good day time opportunities needs to be part of the community care planning process. Front-line day service staff are essential to this process and should work with care managers to ensure that each person's community care plan accurately reflects their needs and wishes for their life as a whole.

Effective individualised planning creates a very powerful picture of the needs, hopes and wants of individual service users. Put together, the plans provide the basis for your future service plan and show where staff skills and resources need to be directed in order to achieve a service which is genuinely user-led.

Staff training strategy

Whatever person-centred planning system you choose, it is essential that staff are properly trained to focus on people's abilities and support them to make choices and that they work with them individually. Bringing in an external organisation to help with staff development can be useful as long as this is integrated with a continuous training plan which builds staff skills over time. (See Chapter 17 on staff development.)

Look at staff strengths and weaknesses and develop a training strategy which will continue throughout the change process and beyond.

Supported employment

Employment should be a major constituent of the new service and early planning is needed to decide how resources can be transferred to make this happen. There is a serious under-investment in supported employment across the UK. Too many services still treat it as an 'add-on' and allocate just two or three staff in a small agency to serve everyone.

Using old resources in new ways

Staffing

If people with learning difficulties are to be successfully supported in spending their waking hours differently, staff will also need to work in different ways. Job descriptions should call for community bridge-builders, college coaches, job coaches, leisure link-workers and workers who support people in a variety of activities. An important requirement running through all job descriptions will be the ability to support users in making relationships and building their own personal networks. Information from the person-centred plans will identify specific skills that will be needed in the new service.

Patterns of attendance at day services may also change. Some people may continue to want a five-day week service, while others will prefer support at weekends. Contracts of employment will need to reflect these changes to give flexibility to working hours.

A personnel strategy will be required to ensure staff are retrained where necessary and those who wish to move are given support to do so.

Finance

Person-centred plans will lead to changes in the way money is spent on day centres in order to create individualised lifestyles. This will require imaginative new thinking and complex shifts in financial management. Direct payments will give people choice and involve them in deciding who gives them support. Individualising the funding to match it to the service user is one of the real opportunities in the re-design of day services. Without these individualised opportunities, a change in the culture of the organisation is very difficult to achieve. Seek allies in your finance department and work with them to make this happen.

A neighbourhood audit

A good understanding of the businesses and services of your local community will reveal opportunities you can exploit. Your neighbourhood may need a local shop, a child-care centre, a printing and photocopying service, a sandwich round for the local industrial estate or a washing and ironing service. Use your local authority business development department to help identify new business opportunities. Check out staff knowledge – many are well connected in the community.

Working closely with local employers and those who understand the needs of the local community can really shift the culture from one which contains people to one which helps them find their potential to participate and contribute.

Stick with it!

This initial stage will feel exciting, frightening and overwhelming. You will be swamped with information and a myriad of important tasks which need to be done at the same time. Keep a clear vision of where you are going, backed up with a practical, step-by-step plan of action plus enthusiastic and committed allies, and you will maintain progress and stay true to your goals.

Changes don't happen overnight because they are tackling society's expectations about the needs of people with disabilities and the extent to which society itself is prepared to change to include them. Tapping into people's creativity, their humanity and the belief that every person has the right to citizenship in their own community will, over time, achieve the desired results.

Focusing on supported living

SUNDERLAND SOCIAL SERVICES closed one of five day centres in 1995 and some of the revenue saved was reinvested in services. Additional staffing was provided to help people who lived in local authority small residential homes get involved in day and evening activities without having to go to a day centre. Staff were specially trained to provide individualised day opportunities and were helped to think differently about how they worked with individuals.

People began to take part in a wide range of different activities throughout the day and evening. They were also given a more 'ordinary life' pattern and encouraged to help in domestic activities such as doing their own laundry, ironing and cooking which had previously been done by staff.

There is a rolling programme of training that ensures the same basic values run throughout the service and people have a common approach to helping individuals. Substantial investment has been made in services that provide an alternative to traditional day centres. Workline, a supported employment agency, enables people to take up open employment. Avenues to Opportunities provides one-to-one support for people to take part in recreation and leisure opportunities. A theatre workshop offers 25 places a day for those interested in the performing arts. A nursery garden has been established for 25 people who are interested in horticulture. Investing in extra staff in the special care units in Sunderland has meant that people who attend these units now have more opportunities to go out and use ordinary community facilities.

Closing a day centre enabled some of the staff to transfer to other services while others took early retirement or redundancy packages. Another innovation for Sunderland Social Services was the employment of a team of welfare benefit advisors. They discovered that many people were not receiving correct benefits and did a valuable service by increasing their incomes and thus their ability to have greater choice of activities. EEC money funded some of these new initiatives.

All these developments have been established after detailed consultation with people who use services and their carers. This is still a major feature of the way services are managed in Sunderland and has contributed greatly to the successful changes that have been made. ■

Contact: John Fisher, Adult Care Manager (Direct Services), Sunderland Social Services, 50 Fawcett Street, Sunderland SR1 1RF. Tel: 0191 553 1000.

Nearly four years and still working on it!
London Borough of Hackney

IN 1994, THE LONDON BOROUGH of Hackney reviewed its day service for people with learning difficulties. The core of the service was three day centres attended by 120 people, many for five days a week. The total cost of the service was £1,130,000. The review included consultation with people who use the service as well as staff and carers. The key aims were:

- to become more person-centred

- to improve assessment and care planning

- to support people to live more ordinary lives in the community.

In March 1995, the social services committee approved further work to create a detailed plan for the future. This resulted in a five-year strategy, the key characteristics of which were:

- the oldest and most inadequate building should be closed in January 1998. People would use a variety of opportunities in the community while still having some contact with the remaining two day centres

- each person using the service should have an individual plan which would then feed into a master plan showing what the service should look like in the future

- new job descriptions for staff would be devised to take account of the needs and wishes of people using the service

- all current jobs would be deleted and staff would have to re-apply for the new ones

- it was clear that some staff might prefer to become redundant rather than be involved in this new type of service. Staff were offered redundancy payments which decreased over a six-month period to encourage early departure

- the new jobs related to specific areas of activity that included individual support workers, performing arts, creative arts, sports, fitness and outdoor pursuits, food and drink, homes and gardens, citizenship and speaking up

- project teams would cover each of these areas and work in the community as well as in the two remaining day centres. The shift would be increasingly towards community involvement

- there would be a large investment in supported employment

- the key aim was to give as much individualised support as possible and for people to have individual timetables

- each individual should have a named key worker who would take the lead role in reviewing and updating the person's plan

- risk assessment would be part of each person's profile so that users, carers and staff could sign up to an agreed level of risk for each individual.

How it works – the process in a nutshell
London Borough of Hackney

Stage 1:   February 1994 – March 1995

Review of social services in-house provision for adults with learning difficulties

↓

Statement of intent to develop 'A New Sense of Direction'

Stage 2:   April 1995 – July 1996

Development of detailed plans to achieve the new direction

↓

5-year plan to improve day opportunities and provision

Stage 3:   August 1996 – June 1997

Putting the framework in place

↓

Reorganisation of in-house service and development of new independent sector provision

Stage 4:   July 1997 – June 1998

'Doing it' – launching changes and supporting new ways of working

↓

Things start to be different for more people

Stage 5:   September 1998 – March 1999

'Seeing it through' – continuing to improve/develop provision

↓

Monitoring outcomes and achieving other planned developments

Stage 6:   April 1999 onward

Extending the 5-year plan

↓

Ensuring that provision keeps improving and moving forward

Employment in the community

CHESHIRE COUNTY COUNCIL Social Services Department has been working for four years to develop supported employment services. So far they have:

- 450 people in employment earning an average wage of £2.75 hourly
- 40 staff providing the supported employment service

- demonstrated the importance of care managers giving priority to supported employment within the assessment procedure
- emphasised the need for core funding to develop supported employment (EEC money should be used for development only)
- piloted an NVQ qualification in job coaching: 180 students completed the programme in 1998

- learned that individuals who work more than 10 hours weekly quickly decrease their use of day centres
- highlighted the importance of helping young people to expect employment as a normal outcome from education
- degrees of disability do not necessarily affect the chances of getting a job. ■

*Contact: John Bottomley, Central Offices, Chester Road, Hartford, Cheshire CW8 2AB
Tel: 01606 301027.*

References

1. Department of Health. *Social Care for Adults with Learning Disabilities (Mental Handicap)*. Circular (92) 15. Jordan: Department of Health, 1992.

2. Department of Health. *Inspection of Day Services for people with a mental handicap. Individual programmes and plans.* London: Department of Health, 1989.

Further reading

Greasley P. Individual planning with adults who have learning difficulties; key issues and key sources. *Disability and Society* 1995; 10:353–62.

Mount B. *Making Futures Happen: A manual for facilitators of personal futures planning.* St Paul (MN): Governor's Planning Council on Developmental Disabilities, 1990.

Murphy T, Rogan P. Closing the Shop: Conversion from sheltered to integrated work. Baltimore: Paul H Brookes Publishing Co. Inc., 1995

O'Brien J. A Guide to Lifestyle Planning. In: Wilcox B, Bellamy GT (eds). *A Comprehensive Guide to the Activities Catalogue: An alternative curriculum for youth and adults with severe disabilities.* Baltimore: Paul H Brookes, 1987.

Chapter 3

Staying on track

It is not easy to produce good, lasting change in services. People are seldom clear about the changes they want; there is often a lot of resistance from all sorts of vested interests; things never work out exactly as planned; key people change jobs at crucial stages; there is never enough money; and if you manage to overcome all these obstacles, the chances are that someone will announce a major reorganisation!

It is vital therefore that you keep going when things get tough – when people become discouraged, when enthusiasm starts to ebb away. Members of the Herefordshire Changing Days Action Learning Set identified three important ingredients:

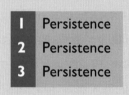

1	Persistence
2	Persistence
3	Persistence

Ways to keep on track

- Hold regular progress meetings

- Celebrate successes with your colleagues – dwell on the good things that have happened

- Incorporate 'problem people' (people who may sabotage your ideas) into your stakeholder group. It is better to work with them than to have them acting independently

- If you get stuck, look for external support or consultancy. Outside people can often see things you might miss. Organisations such as the NDT provide external consultancy and can often be used as troubleshooters

- Keep in touch with others who are trying to individualise services. It often helps to discuss problems with people in a similar situation who may have found solutions that can help

Suggestions for getting personal support

- Identify someone you feel comfortable with and ask them to meet you at regular intervals, say monthly, for support
- Do you have a network of people you can turn to when things get tough?
- Can you keep in regular contact with others who are tackling similar issues, for example through an action learning group?
- Regularly take stock of your achievements
- Consider persuading your employer to buy in external support or consultancy

Get personal support

People who are taking a lead in making things happen are usually involved in a wide range of activities. Life can get hectic and it is easy to feel overwhelmed or depressed, especially when things don't go according to plan. Make sure you get personal support.

This can come from a variety of people. You may be able to talk things over with your boss, a colleague who is not directly involved, a partner at home, a friend who is interested or someone from another organisation who is facing similar challenges. It is important that this person is there for *you*, so if your boss is one of the sources of your stress, don't choose him or her as a personal supporter! Set up a mutually supportive arrangement with a colleague. Agree to meet once a month for two hours. Take an hour each to talk over any problems while the other person acts as consultant. Just having someone who can ask the right questions very often is enough to get you through a difficult patch.

When someone is acting as a supporter, it is important they do not try and solve your problems for you, or even tell you what to do. They should ask questions and encourage you to think of solutions. They may also help you see your achievements. It is easy to lose sight of achievements when overwhelmed by problems.

Get personal support from an external agency. Some organisations will agree to pay for this, particularly if you are a lone worker with no obvious or natural supports within your own organisation.

Quality and evaluation

This is not the place for a lengthy discussion on how to measure quality and evaluate services. However, there are some issues concerning quality which are directly related to making things happen. In particular, there are ways of looking at the quality of a service which:

- focus on what is happening to people who are using the service – their experience of life
- involve local stakeholders so that they learn from a review of quality
- lead to practical steps which will help the service to improve.

The NDT has carried out a number of person-centred service reviews. These involve a small team of local stakeholders who each spend time with one person using the service. After several hours with one person over a week, the team member gains a very rich picture of that person's life and the impact of the service upon them. By bringing together the experiences of all team members, it is possible to learn a great deal about the service, where it is succeeding and any priorities for change. This sort of exercise often provides a useful opportunity to get senior managers to speak to people who use the services.

The British Institute for Learning Disabilities and the NDT are collaborating in a project which explores this sort of approach as a means of encouraging services to look continuously at their quality and take steps to improve it. *The Quality Is Our Business Too** project is looking at the idea of a national accreditation scheme based on the principle of continuous quality improvement. One useful feature of this project is the work carried out by Martin Cattermole in developing a set of easy-to-understand outcome measures. These are devised from discussions with people with learning difficulties and some family members. They are based on ten statements of outcome:

1   I make choices about my daily lifestyle
2   I make decisions about my life
3   I take part in everyday activities and get help to do this if I need it
4   People listen to me and treat me with respect
5   I have friendships and relationships
6   I participate alongside ordinary members of the community
7   I get the chance to do a paid job and the help I need to do it well
8   I am safe from harassment and abuse
9   I make plans for the future
10 My family have a say about the services I receive

---

* Martin Cattermole, Oxfordshire Learning Disability NHS Trust, P.O. Chambers, Market Square, Witney, Oxton OX8 6LN. Tel: 01993 774045. Fax: 01993 709128.

Quality reviews of this type can be a positive experience for those who take part in them and provide useful information on how to move forward in developing a service. Conducted in a positive and constructive way, they can be one of the things that keep you motivated and on target.

Chapter 4

Strategic planning and commissioning

Vision and Principles

To achieve effective strategic planning and commissioning we need:

- Clear and shared values
- Planning for each individual
- Flexible budgets
- Commitment to joint working
- Planning for a person's whole life
- Flexible contracting arrangements
- Clear service specifications ■

The introduction of the NHS and Community Care Act in 1993 has brought about many new labels and structures for services and those who work in them. Before the community care changes, the activities we now call 'commissioning' and 'purchasing' often went on, but not necessarily under those names.

What do we mean by commissioning?

We mean:

- finding out what people want in terms of how they live
- finding out what help they need to do this
- using funding and organising skills to ensure that people get the necessary supports
- keeping in touch with people to make sure that it still makes sense.

Described like this, it sounds simple. Yet so often the structures and systems to control funding, maintain existing services and establish equity and accountability, actually make the process very difficult and complicated. This need not be the case if action is built on the following starting points.

Clear and shared values

It is essential to have a very clear and strong set of person-centred values that recognises the uniqueness of each individual. One way of better understanding this is to ask the following questions:

- Do people with learning difficulties have similar opportunities to the rest of society?
- Do people with learning difficulties have a similar variety of lifestyles as the rest of society?

These are important objectives. All people involved in services – from directors to support staff – need to learn more about and thoroughly understand these values.

Planning for each individual

We must not make assumptions about men and women with learning difficulties based upon some idea of what 'people like them need'. We must work with each person to find out what is most important for him or her and the planning must match our values and aims. Many people are using Personal Futures Planning, Essential Lifestyle Planning and PATH to do this. (See Chapter 7.)

All of these forms of person-centred planning recognise the uniqueness of the individual, have community inclusion as an explicit aim and ensure that the person with learning disabilities and those who know him or her best have the most powerful voice. This type of planning also emphasises action: as well as finding out what people want, action plans are developed to ensure they get it.

Flexible budgets

Funding is directly related to individual people and should not be tied inappropriately into long-term inflexible block contracts. Block contracts mean that most people with learning difficulties will be pigeon-holed into whatever service is already funded. If we plan for individuals, we must ensure the flexibility of funding to respond.

One problem is that most areas have funding tied up in large day centres. Another is that funding is tied up in residential services for people who have been resettled from long-stay hospitals. Ways of freeing up funding are listed in the box.

Making funding feasible

- Using a small amount of bridging money to start the process of change

- Separating out the day support contract and budget where a service is contracted to provide both residential and day supports

- Bringing people back from expensive out-of-area placements and ring-fencing any savings for bridging funding

- While using person-centred planning, commissioning for a group of people with similar needs and wishes, i.e. reproviding a large enough part of a traditional service to free up funding for a new pattern of support (e.g. supported employment service)

- Getting social services, health and education working together to ensure the most efficient and effective use of funding

Commitment to joint working

Change in services is rarely achieved through the actions of one organisation alone. Effective change comes about through strong alliances and good collaborative working. Many people believe this is the responsibility of health and social services, but it goes way beyond this. This partnership is indeed important, but the issue of collaboration is far more complex and wide-ranging.

Support is required to create alliances and collaboration between people with learning disabilities, carers, service providers and purchasers. They need common aims, quick and easy decision-making processes, shared training opportunities and long-term commitment to see change through. Change seldom occurs or is sustained with short-term efforts.

It is important for health and social services to have effective joint commissioning procedures. If these are in place, then it is possible to take advantage of funding opportunities and people are less likely to fall through the net.

Planning for a person's whole life

Supported living[1] is a way of ensuring that people have the lives they want: leading their own chosen lifestyle, living with whom they choose, living where they want, doing what they want, choosing who supports them and how they are supported. It is often misunderstood as 'another residential service option'.

Anyone involved in promoting supported living quickly realises that it is far more than just finding a home for someone. Supported living raises people's expectations about determining their own life – in all its aspects. When people have their own homes, they develop raised expectations about what to do during the day. Better days raise their expectations about their home life. We must be prepared for this and adjust our planning processes accordingly. We are used to developing neat service entities but must not plan people's lives along the same lines.

Flexible contracting arrangements

Contracting can be exciting! And if we are doing our jobs properly, it will be. Commissioners need to use contracting to ensure that people get what they need and want, that providers have space and opportunity for creativity, and that there are positive incentives for helping women and men with learning difficulties get what they need and want.

Examples of this are listed in the box opposite.

Flexible contracting

- Separate out contracts to include a core element for infrastructure (to give stability to the provider) and have individual contracts for people's specific support needs

- Contract with separate organisations for the provision of residential supports and the provision of day supports

- Contract for and fund outcomes in supported employment, i.e. paying for the successful development of a job for a person and continuing payments for sustaining them in that job. Of course, these must be jobs that people want and enjoy!

- Stimulate development of providers and services, what some may call 'managing the market'. This requires a good knowledge of what is needed and the best ways to deliver it and requires far more sophistication than just always doing a straightforward open tender. New types of service often need to be supported, nurtured and pump-primed

Clear service specifications

Commissioners and purchasers must ensure that they have clear specifications in place. General service specifications are needed for different types of service as well as complementary service specifications for each person. This emphasises the need for good person-centred planning, as it is the framework from which the individual specification should emerge.

If specifications are to work, they must be living documents which are easy to understand, have clearly defined outcomes for the individual and establish recognisable standards. The specification will be separate to the contract, but an important annexed part of it. Contracts are often phrased in legal-speak, but it is important for the specification to be referred to regularly and therefore understood by all. This can be achieved only by using simple everyday language.

Staying involved

Commissioners and purchasers need to find ways of becoming involved and staying involved with people and their services. This enables more honesty about the immediate situation. Seeing things at first hand and understanding people's real life experiences, makes it much more difficult to gloss over or ignore something that needs changing. Some common ways of keeping in touch are:

- develop a relationship with just one person who has learning disabilities, either formally or informally
- set up and get involved with service reviews that involve spending time with people
- have meetings for feedback and regular consultation with people who are using services.

Effective commissioning

- Establish flexibility with contracts and funding
- Nurture and develop good providers
- Take action against poor quality providers
- Be interventionist and 'hands on'
- Promote and support service development activities
- Work very closely with people who have learning disabilities and providers.
- Promote mutual relationships

Guard against . . .

- assuming that big is cheap and small is expensive (it's not!)
- bringing people together on the basis of a shared label or diagnosis
- omitting to check back with people to see if what they are getting still makes sense for them
- maintaining the status quo because it is an easier short-term option (in the long-term it does not work)
- becoming obsessed with activity rather than outcomes for people

Positive roles for commissioners

- Make people with learning disabilities more powerful
- Connect people with learning disabilities to their communities more effectively
- Develop services based upon good person-centred planning

Involving users and carers

User and carer involvement is a safeguard against joint commissioning becoming a process of inward-looking bureaucracy. They should be involved in identifying need and providing input to monitoring and review. Commissioning authorities should be clear about the overall process, and the role of users and carers within it.

From: *An Introduction to Joint Commissioning.* Department of Health: 1995.

The five stages of the commissioning cycle differentiate between type and level of activities.

Strategic framework

- Establish a common view of required future developments
- Establish shared values and broad strategic objectives
- Clarify individual agency roles and responsibilities

Strategic planning

- Complete strategic needs assessment
- Identify existing services and resources
- Define priorities and agree outcomes
- Consult users, carers and providers
- Agree commissioning intentions

Operational planning

- Establish contracting mechanisms
- Develop quality assurance requirements
- Undertake market management and provider development activities
- Establish infrastructure needs

Purchasing activities

- Agree service specifications
- Select providers
- Agree contracts and monitoring arrangements

Monitoring and review

- Collect performance information
- Review provider performance standards
- Review/renegotiate contracts
- Feed information back into strategic review

Different individuals and agencies must be involved in different parts of the commissioning cycle. Not all need to be involved throughout.

The commissioning cycle provides a framework within which the planning and commissioning timetables of the different agencies (health, housing and social care) can be brought together.[2]

Conclusion

Only when a large number of people have lifestyles similar to the rest of the population can we truly claim significant achievement.

However, we must not be daunted by the size of the task: we have to begin somewhere. That starting point must be to achieve something better and different for a small number of people (perhaps just one person), learn from it and then use the experience to do more. Staying close to men and women with learning difficulties is the only way to be in touch and to maintain the integrity to see such complex change through.

References

1. Kinsella P. *Supported Living. A new paradigm.* Manchester: National Development Team, 1993.

2. Department of Health. *An Introduction to Joint Commissioning.* London: Department of Health, 1995.

Further reading

Fielder B, Twitchin D. *Achieving User Participation: Planning services for people with severe physical and sensory disabilities.* London: King's Fund, 1992.

Greig R. Joint commissioning: searching for stability in an unstable world. In: *Tizard Learning Disability Review* 1997; 2(1).

Waddington P. Joint commissioning of services for people with learning disabilities: a review of the principles and the practice. In: *British Journal of Learning Disabilities* 1995; 23.

Chapter 5

Getting a life, not a building

Vision and Principles

> *Changing Days is about how we move from our buildings-based, service-led model to an almost invisible needs-led approach that supports people in the real world of our communities.* (Changing Days, 1996)

For some time now, services have been moving away from complete reliance on special buildings, with many people with learning difficulties spending a lot of time out and about in the community. More areas are setting up services with just an office as a base with people using ordinary buildings which everyone uses. Some areas have already closed one or more day centres. Others are planning to do so. The goal eventually is to achieve services which can support people with whatever help they need, in the same range of places that everyone else uses – for work, learning and leisure activities. ■

Using buildings differently

There will be a period for the majority of services when some traditional day centre buildings are still in use but this does not mean that change is delayed. For example, checking out your local neighbourhood (see Chapter 2, Getting Started) may reveal a need for a community centre and your day centre building might just be the perfect place, thus becoming a focal point for the whole community. Staff at one day centre sited near a main street realised that creating a new doorway in one wall provided easy access to space which could be turned into a coffee shop. This is now a popular refreshment spot for local people as well as providing a variety of new opportunities for centre users.

Funding from a Single Regeneration Budget on the Trowbridge Estate in the London Borough of Hackney will be used to change the focus of the Trowbridge Centre, a conventional day centre for people with learning difficulties. It will become a community resource for all by:

- offering space for community groups and activities which people with learning difficulties can also join
- working with the local community to identify their needs and respond by running small businesses such as a cafe or photocopying service, which could provide employment opportunities.

Thus it will make people with learning difficulties better off financially as well as find valued roles in a setting where they receive support but also contribute to their local community.

When the closure of a day centre is being discussed, the most frequent response of people using the centre is: *'Where will I meet my friends?'* Perhaps it is a sad reflection on services that the question should even need to be asked. Such a question should eventually become unnecessary as people will be meeting friends in the same places as the rest of society. In the meantime, services are responding to this problem in different ways. Club houses and drop-in centres are currently popular solutions. However, care needs to be taken that such ventures do not become miniature versions of day centres, with the same disadvantages. It will be easier to prevent segregation and isolation if a meeting place is part of an ordinary community complex such as a neighbourhood, leisure or community centre – a place with a variety of uses for the general public as well as for those with learning difficulties. Such a setting will also present more opportunities for people to link with and contribute to other activities in the building.

Working without a 'day centre' base

A number of services have already been established which only use ordinary facilities in the community and operate from a small office. Sometimes they have come about because a day centre has closed and resources have been rechannelled, and in other cases they have been set up especially for people with complex needs, many of whom previously had no service. In the latter case they often support small numbers of people and not necessarily on a five-day-a-week basis for each person.

What this demonstrates is that working without a traditional day centre can result in a much more ordinary and inclusive lifestyle for the women and men they support. It means that some people have already arrived at the point where we are striving for them to be – in the community. In the community it can rain, turn cold, you can wait ages for a bus, people can be rude and people can be kind. But it is in the community where the widest range of opportunities are to be found, where the greatest number of relationships can be formed and where there is a diversity of cultures.

Granted, it is not all plain sailing. There are challenges to be faced, including the important one of the 'respite care' element of the service, but not having a base means that you just have to get on with finding solutions: you really get to know a person, discover their interests, see them in different environments and find acceptable alternative back-ups. Experience shows that 'not having a special base to go to' is not such a problem as might be imagined. As one manager said: *'As a very last resort we will use the office, but it's not usually a problem'.*

Advantages of a non-buildings based service	Disadvantages of day centre model
• You can take advantage of the full range of opportunities available in the community	• More limited choices available
• Staff learn new skills and learn what support they actually do need	• It encourages the 'readiness' approach. Users, and staff, practising skills which may not be what's needed out in the community
• Fosters a get-on-with-it approach – encourages problem-solving and creativity	• It may lessen creativity. It can quickly become the first line for cover arrangements and easier to fall back on in bad weather
• Develops a better sense of what is doable because you are out there in the community doing it	• It removes ordinariness
• People may get a new perspective on what home should be, when it should be accessible	• It limits contact between carers and staff – staff and users meet at day centre rather than from home
• Chance to be in a multi-cultural environment. More opportunities to reinforce identification with one's own culture; link with supporters from similar backgrounds	• More difficult to meet people's cultural and identity needs
• Many more opportunities to form relationships with ordinary members of the public	• Staff can gravitate towards it. It can be seen more as a place for staff rather than people with learning difficulties
• More flexible working hours, including evenings and weekends	• Day centre open only at certain times
• More chance that you will meet people with things in common (e.g. interests, memberships); more chance to become a contributor	• Rather than being a stepping stone, you may never get out!

Kevin is a young man in his thirties. He lives at home with his mother and when first linked with the service, had no regular activities and a very limited social circle. He had not received any services for fifteen years. He had no eye contact, no speech and a hearing loss. He could understand small words and his mother wrote simple words down for him.

On joining the service, he had a lot of help with speech and language and much support from a clinical psychologist. A communications system placing symbols alongside words was devised for him and he began making real choices about what he wanted to do.

Kevin particularly enjoys art and has joined mainstream art and pottery classes at his local college. He has begun going out for cups of coffee and snacks with some of his classmates. He took to using a computer keyboard with remarkable ease and now has a Litewriter through which he can hold conversations with people using typed messages. This device attracts much interest! He goes swimming regularly and visits a neighbour whose house he found very interesting.

Perhaps the highlight of Kevin's achievements was an exhibition of his artwork and pottery at the cafe where he has become a regular. Family and friends came to see the exhibition and his picture was in the local newspaper. Kevin's keyworker is currently looking into employment opportunities for him.

Planning

Logistics, accountability and communication become even more important when a team is largely out and about, away from the office. It is essential that plans are clearly recorded, including details such as times, contacts, support needs and ways of travelling. It is important that others in the team are aware of people's plans, their routines, their families and other contacts. Having 'seconds' named as back-ups who will know the person and his or her family well is valuable for planning, cover, staff support and strengthening confidence in the service.

Management style

The service should be managed in a way which is enabling and empowering and is based on democratic decision-making. A prescriptive management style, directional or hierarchical, will not work. Staff must be able to act on their own initiative, take charge in a crisis and manage their own time and workload. Because they are the public face of the service, it is essential that they feel they have an investment in making it work and have contributed to all its policies. The quality of their support is crucial to the person they are supporting and will not happen if they do not believe in what they are doing, or if they feel isolated and unsupported. Much of their work is invisible to the manager and colleagues so trust, too, is important.

The manager must also be physically present in the office. Workers' time is likely to be more scheduled than the manager's so workers must be able to grab ten minutes of manager time when needed. The manager must make a priority of nurturing a team of strong, competent and effective workers. It is essential that people can ask for support to offload and know that support is not far away.

It is also important to create a learning organisation. Ideas may or may not come from outside so the team needs to generate and implement their own ideas. They should be happy to explore ideas and take risks and all team members should feel responsible for the development of the service.

Staffing

Staff need to be supporters, enablers, bridge-builders and link makers. They need to be strong, confident and prepared to pioneer. They must be able to discover a person's gifts, even when these are difficult to see; to take a glimmer of interest and build on it.

Employing sessional workers with special skills or from minority backgrounds can make it easier to meet particular individual and cultural needs. A Muslim man supported by a fellow Muslim can now go to the mosque. A Black male user, previously supported by a woman, was linked with a Black male sessional worker, and can now fit into and be accepted at the local snooker club.

Training in different cultures and religions will make staff more confident and creative about offering culturally specific opportunities with whatever support is appropriate.

Staff skills and approaches

- Confident, resourceful and work on their own initiative
- Bridge-builders
- Community developers
- People who know the community
- Strong belief in people
- Cope with a crisis
- Enjoy being with the person
- Enabling
- Modelling

Cover

In order for users and carers to be confident about the service, it is essential to provide effective cover for time off, such as holidays, but also for unexpected events such as sudden illness. This is particularly important in the early days when relationships are being established, when parents and carers may be nervous about what the service can deliver, and staff themselves are unused to working away from a base.

Arranging back-up

- Build up a pool of sessional workers who know the people using the service

- Offer support at an alternative time of the week

- Ensure that the manager is available to provide back-up

- Arrange staff administrative time so there is always one member of the team in the office able to cover at short notice

- In the event of illness, ensure that staff agree to call each other or the manager at home – out of hours, if necessary – to increase chance of cover being arranged

Support for staff

As with planning, support becomes even more important in a service where staff spend most of their time out and about, working on their own. They must think on their feet, change plans as needed and sometimes deal with difficult situations. There will be times when the job is creative and invigorating, but there will also be times of stress and tension. It is important to use formal supports as effectively as possible but new ways of working require new ways of thinking about worker support.

Support can take the form of:

- supervision
- team meetings
- linking informally with colleagues
- having office time in order to see colleagues
- phone-link support
- named 'seconds' so that at least two people know the person and his or her family well and can help each other in planning, feedback and approaches to supporting.

Support for sessional workers

Sessional workers are even more likely to feel remote from the rest of the team and it is essential to devise ways that they can be part of the support system. Working in isolation makes it harder for them to try new ideas and search for different opportunities and they are likely to fall back on safe options. Workers must have a very clear programme with clear objectives and careful planning towards achieving those objectives.

Support from elsewhere

It can be difficult for an innovative team to find appropriate support and advice from outside. As pioneers, you will have other people seeking your help, wanting to visit and asking you to speak at conferences.

It is useful to create links with other agencies and organisations who may be working in different ways but from a similar standpoint – for example, supported employment and circles of support.

Support may also come from people you see daily such as carers, the person concerned, fellow students in a class, colleagues at a work site. The people who see you in action are likely not to be your manager or colleagues but members of the public.

Kingsthorpe Lighthouse
Cambridgeshire Social Services

THE CREATION OF THE 'Lighthouse' was one of those rare moments in large organisations when, for a few, service development exactly matched people's needs at that particular moment.

It all started when, for various different reasons, a small number of people found themselves together at a large multi-purpose day centre. Some had spent up to twenty years at a local adult training centre. Others, due to difficulties in their personal life, had been placed at the centre because no other more suitable resource had been available. It was clear that although these people had very differing aspirations and skills, they were linked by a common thread of boredom with the existing service.

To begin changing this situation, two crucial decisions were made. The first was to assign a half-time worker to work only with these individuals. The second was to re-negotiate the cleaning contract at the centre to gain approximately £4,000 for the group to do with as they wished.

For the first six months the worker concentrated *only* on supporting people to develop skills in areas which were directly useful in general community life such as lateral thinking, problem-solving, making choices, building relationships. During this period, the worker also focused on supporting families and carers. In fact, one third of the time was spent in this activity and this intensive input resulted in families remaining consistently supportive even though at times it was extremely difficult emotionally.

People were soon spending more and more time away from the centre accessing on their own a whole range of activities which no professional could ever have imagined. The money mentioned above had been divided to give each person £500 per year. It was also clear that the centre as a base was becoming a major hindrance and so a bungalow belonging to the department in the city centre was gained and then furnished using slippage from the staffing budget.

One and a half full-time equivalent staff members now support over thirty people from The Lighthouse. Many people from the original group are now living in their own homes and several have formed long-term relationships.

The cost to the department is approximately £1,200 per year per person, which is about one third of the original placement cost at the day centre. ■

Contact: Mark Douglas, Milbury Care Services, 2 Queen Street, Lichfield, Staffs. WS13 6QD. Tel: 01543 415 106.

What do workers get paid for?

It seems a daft question but one that is likely to come up in a non-buildings-based service. There are no easy answers about where the boundaries of paid work begin and end.

It is good to match users and workers who have similar interests and passions. There is nothing worse than being supported by someone who clearly does not enjoy your favourite activity – and vice versa! A member of staff who is already keen on amateur dramatics is much more likely to be successful in helping someone develop their interest in drama. They will know more about the drama scene, what is going on and likely people to link with. However, should we pay staff to support the person to go to the drama group? It is essential to share a good time with someone. You will see people relaxed and enthused and when you note how they react in different environments, you will change your own perception of them and they of you. You will develop trust. But, should we pay staff for supporting someone to go out for a meal and then on to the theatre?

These are difficult questions. Clearly we are looking for long-term, sustainable relationships and real community involvement. One-off activities leave us unclear whether we are acting as friends or staff. Look carefully at the goals for each person. How will these be achieved and in what timescale? Staff must agree where and how to place the boundaries; how to get the right balance between maintaining valuable flexibility and creating positive ways of developing relationships between staff and the men and women they support.

Linking with family and carers

Increased contact with people's families is a distinct advantage in a non-buildings-based service. Meeting people at their home each day means that staff get to know families and carers more easily and intimately and develop an accurate feel for a person's identity. Working flexibly provides greater opportunity to give added support that links people in with family and cultural activities and reconnects and strengthens family ties.

Making it work for people with complex needs

It is easy for those who plan services to anticipate that we will always need a different type of service for men and women with more complex needs. But if planning begins at an individual level and appropriate support is provided, with each obstacle tackled as it arises, there is no reason why those with the most complex needs and behaviours cannot be supported in the community. A growing number of examples, including from the field of supported employment, demonstrate how people respond positively to ordinary environments and learn from those around them. There can be some resistance from members of the public but mostly people accept and often welcome the person's presence and contribute new ideas about what they could do.

Most important is that people are well supported, that workers are positive and confident, that all support needs have been considered and that successful ventures can be undertaken that will increase confidence and can be built upon.

Ellen was 19 when first linked to the service, had just finished school and was not receiving any other services. She had considerable behavioural difficulties, was very withdrawn and would not leave her house at all.

After spending time getting to know Ellen, staff discovered the trigger for her challenging behaviour. She became very upset if spoken to in a complex or long-winded way. Simple, monosyllabic statements worked best. Ellen's behaviour changed and she began responding much more positively. Use of a method known as 'thank you for saying no' when she refused something was very helpful.

The breakthrough in working out how to communicate with Ellen enabled staff to progress to encouraging her to go outside the house. This was achieved by using a ball game which gradually persuaded her to go nearer the front door and eventually outside.

Initially, Ellen's outings were restricted to a local park and cafe because she would only travel on buses of a particular colour and would only walk certain routes. Routes are still a challenge for her but Ellen and the staff have made substantial progress. The most impressive example of this involved introducing Ellen to a particular route (which did involve a bus journey) in stages and then taking her for a brief daytime visit to a jazz club – the goal of the outing. After further intensive work, she was able to enjoy an evening at the club.

Ellen now attends college classes regularly and although there are still occasional outbursts, she enjoys interactions with other people and has a wider range of activities.

Staying focused

If the team is based within a wider service such as a local authority, there is a risk that the aims and principles of the service may be diluted. Other demands on staff time such as working with groups or staff training, may make it difficult to maintain a genuine one-to-one service. Financial pressures, in conflict with other service needs, may also lessen the quality of the work. A secure focused future is the only way such services can confidently develop. Monitoring them is obviously important, for innovative services require a strong platform from which to take risks. The service must have clear goals for itself and a strong value-base from which to make decisions. Team agreement is essential.

The richest place for opportunities lies in the community but it is important to plan clearly with people in mind and monitor what is actually happening: for example, are more men pursuing employment? Are people in gender-stereotyped roles? We must continue to ask these questions and justify what we are supporting each person to do.

Costing the service

We need new and different ways of costing this type of service (see Chapter 16). It can seem very expensive if it is costed on the number of hours of direct support a person receives. But a full cost-benefit analysis is needed over a long period to account for 'unseen' benefits such as:

- the value of being reconnected with or spending more time with family or others as a result of those people seeing the person with 'new eyes', that is more capable, more valued, possessing gifts and abilities
- more efficient planning and linking with other services as a result of increased knowledge of the person and their circumstances
- improved quality of life
- becoming a contributory member of a local community
- being a consumer of local resources and goods
- if working, being a tax payer and less dependent on benefits.

Words of caution

It can be difficult to come up with the goods when faced with:

- exhaustion
- watering down of ideas and principles
- pressure to succeed
- over-reliance on one or two key people
- pressures on what the role involves (e.g. are you a care manager, health visitor?)
- criticism of expense
- isolation
- service seen as an indulgence.

But it is worth it!

Chapter 6

Creating inclusive communities

Vision and Principles

A vision of inclusiveness will demand major shifts in the way we think and act – as individuals, in organisations and as members of our local communities. The challenge for all of us is to create communities based on co-operation and interdependence, where everyone is seen as having a contribution to make and where people's differences are acknowledged and valued rather than being a reason for rejecting them. (Changing Days, 1996)

Developing inclusion requires:

- commitment from commissioners and providers to make it a priority, not just a fringe activity
- moving beyond segregated group activity in the community
- recruiting staff who have good connections with their community
- secure, continuous funding
- building social networks to be an integral part of planning with individuals
- sensible but flexible risk policies which don't inhibit someone's opportunities for new relationships and new experiences
- non-bureaucratic volunteer recruitment procedures
- understanding that inclusion means a partnership with ordinary citizens – community is people not places.

Commitment to full inclusion of people with learning difficulties in the wider community regardless of disability should be part of the service's vision for the future, understood and practised by everyone. The philosophy of inclusion must be embedded in every part of the organisation. ■

Friendships and relationships

For most of us, relationships in all their variety – one-to-one relationships, neighbours, friends made through leisure pursuits, club memberships, religious connections – are one of the most important aspects of our lives. People with learning difficulties are no different. When a day centre is closing, one of the most common concerns is, 'How will I keep in touch with my friends?' 'How can I make new friends?' Yet services, by and large, have given very little attention to this fundamental human need. We have become quite sophisticated in helping people with daily living skills and vocational skills but have given a great deal more attention to bed-making and budgeting than we have to befriending. We are helping people to be competent but they are still alone.

From community presence to community connections

Many women and men with learning difficulties are now getting out and about to a wide range of places in the community – leisure centres, colleges, pubs, shops, cafes and restaurants. But much of this is group activity rather than individual involvement. And it is segregated – special classes at the community centre or college rather than integrated classes with other students, or swimming only at special sessions for disabled people. Very often people have an extremely busy week, packed with activities. But how many of these provide opportunities for making real community connections and relationships? Often the service system gets in the way again – immediately the class is over, for example, it is quickly out to catch 'the transport' or the person is stuck for getting home.

Focus on opportunities for relationships

In *Friends: A manual for connecting persons with disabilities and community members,*[1] the authors suggest a number of 'connecting strategies' to achieve successful inclusion, which also emphasise the importance of creating opportunities for relationships and not just activities.

Activities can set the stage for meeting people, but some present greater opportunities than others. For example, shopping centres are great for 'people watching' but they are less effective for 'people meeting'. However, someone who often goes to a neighbourhood cafe accompanied by a member of staff when other 'regulars' are there will create a familiarity that may lead to a relationship.

Community activities can mean taking seven or eight residents out in the group home minibus and stopping at McDonald's, or it could be one staff member taking someone to help at the weekly church coffee morning. The first instance is unlikely to create an opportunity to really get to know anyone but helping at the church coffee morning would.

> John takes his Litewriter (communication aid) everywhere he goes, including regular visits to his local cafe. Curiosity to find out more about this gadget brings people in the cafe over to talk to him.

> When Julie goes swimming, we take fun equipment (large ball, floats, etc.). This has brought people over to join in – adults, not just children!

Building social networks

Extending someone's social network is not always easy. Many men and women with learning difficulties do not have any non-paid people in their lives. Many are separated or distant from their families. Others have been isolated from ordinary community people and experiences through institutionalisation and segregation. For these people, staff and others paid to be with them are the key people in their lives: all their relationships are dependent on the service system. Some members of staff do become good friends but they are rarely given the time or the opportunity to help people gain a wider network of friends outside services.

Using the artificial to get to the ordinary

Working to extend a person's social network can also feel artificial. We say – you can't force friendship, you can't deliberately go about finding friends for people – just let it happen. However, a person who doesn't know how to make friends will need help with friendship. Someone who has been isolated from the community will not know how to set about making connections which might lead to friendship. Sometimes it needs action which may feel artificial to get to the ordinary. Here the kind of support being given is crucial. The person who is supporting a woman or man to make social connections must understand the importance of facilitating rather than taking the lead; ensuring that the person with learning difficulties is the focus, that the facilitator does not become the centre of attention – the one everyone wants to talk to – while the person with disabilities stays out on the edge. The facilitator must know that his/her job is to 'fade' support as soon as possible. As *Changing Days* says: *'Do not hover round the person: show the world that they are their own person. Let them take the initiative and speak for themselves as much as possible'*.

Getting beyond one-to-one

Recognising people's lack of friends and other social relationships, a variety of schemes – citizen and other forms of advocacy, leisure partnerships, befriending schemes – have been working for some years now to overcome social isolation. An underlying feature of much of this work is one-to-one links. Historically this is understandable. When many of these schemes started, even the idea of recognising and treating people with learning difficulties as individuals was new. The need for one-to-one links was acute and concentrating on one-to-one was entirely appropriate at the time in order to shift thinking. Now, however, we have learnt that while one-to-one connections are very important, they are just the first step. We need to guard against the person becoming so reliant on one relationship that if it breaks down – and some will, if this is real life! – the person may end up worse off than before: feeling even more isolated, with diminished self-confidence and little inclination to try friendship again. We must build social networks which will give people the same mix of ties and connections that most of us enjoy. When a volunteer, a befriender, a partner in an advocacy scheme, is linked with a woman or man with learning difficulties, the job is not finished – it has just begun.

The role of volunteers

Volunteers play valuable roles in human service agencies. However, if formal volunteers take the place of more natural relationships, dependence on volunteers as a way of providing genuine relationships can create problems. The 'formal' status of a volunteer can obstruct real friendship. So, too, can the images of dependency sometimes unconsciously be associated with volunteering. The volunteer may feel an obligation rather than just liking and wanting to be with the person. Also, if the formal volunteering agreement ends, there is often little contact afterwards.

How often do volunteer schemes judge success by the number of volunteers helping with segregated clubs or other group activities rather than by the number of friendships begun through a volunteer connection and continued outside the Wednesday club night or the Saturday afternoon bowling session?

It is important for agencies to look carefully at their policies and procedures concerning the use of volunteers. A rigid, bureaucratic recruitment policy will deter a lot of people – staff and potential volunteers – and contradicts the philosophy of promoting friendship.

Lengthy training programmes can also turn volunteers into quasi-professionals and inhibit the development of more natural, ordinary lifestyles and connections. On the whole, training which focuses on helping the volunteer to understand and respond to the needs of the individual person who is being supported has been more effective than all-inclusive volunteer group training based on specific disability topics.

Every effort should be made to encourage volunteers to extend a person's social network. This does not necessarily mean seeking additional commitment from the volunteer or refusing the help of someone with only limited time to spare. But it may mean encouraging them to think differently about a person, to keep network-building at the front of their mind and think creatively about ways to draw someone else into a person's life. Volunteer co-ordinators may be afraid to ask too much lest they put people off, but many volunteers welcome the chance of a deeper, more focused and purposeful commitment to an individual.

Circles of support

A circle of support can help to minimise anxieties about risk and can also address the challenge of developing continuity in a person's life. A circle begins with people the individual knows well and wants to have in his or her circle. New people are introduced to the circle only because they are known to others already in the circle. In this way, the circle builds trust and can be self-regulating. It removes the need for a formal risk assessment and keeps the social network-building more natural.

Paid staff and volunteers tend to come and go. A circle of support aims to build long-term commitment. Of course, as in anyone's social network, people may come and go, but because the circle does not rely on any one person, a stronger sense of continuity is developed and the person's social network is more firmly rooted.

During the course of the Changing Days work, we saw a tremendous amount of interest in, and understanding of, the value of circles in developing people's social networks. Several circles began in Belfast as part of the work of CLASP (Community Living and Support Programme), which is run under the auspices of the parents' organisation, the Orchardville Society. And as part of its resettlement programme, Ely Hospital in Cardiff appointed a worker specifically to develop circles for people leaving the hospital.

Jay Nolen Community Services in Los Angeles transformed its residential services between 1993 and 1996 by assisting more than sixty people with autism to move from hostels into their own homes and apartments and then closed the hostels. Circles of support planned and managed each person's transition and now maintain responsibility for ensuring that people receive adequate services.[2] In the UK the concept is starting to be used to create individual profiles of each service user from which a person-centred service can be developed.

The above are examples of circles both within and outside traditional services. Circles focus on developing the long-term commitment of ordinary unpaid citizens in a person's life. They can be a bridge enabling effective change from traditional services. But they can also lose their focus if they become just another part of a traditional service system. How the unique characteristics of circles of support can and should be safeguarded is an issue which needs a great deal of careful thought and debate.

Planning differently

The appropriate personal involvement in people's lives is support. Thinking in terms of 'support' rather than 'services' will help shift the way we organise and use the human and financial resources we have. The lives of many men and women with learning difficulties are still dominated by professionals and services and this situation will remain until a service becomes genuinely person- and community-centred rather than service-centred. This requires a radical shift in thinking by commissioners and providers. The table on pages 58–59 contrasting different ways of planning is helpful in describing a method of embedding inclusion in the way we think about support for individuals.

Service commitment

Changing Days emphasised the importance of creating an organisational culture committed to full inclusion of people with learning disabilities regardless of their degree of disability. Inclusion will not happen without a major shift in resources, particularly staff time, towards building relationships – in all their variety – with ordinary citizens. This means making inclusion an integral part of the day service strategy – a priority, not just a fringe activity.

Circles of support – a brother's view

My brother's circle has now been running for about two years and from my point of view, it has made some big differences. Andrew is genuinely the focus of attention. It's his circle – he owns it and he knows this is different. He plans the dates, we talk about what he wants to do in the meetings, hold them where he wants to, and do social things that he wants to do. I've never seen him so enthusiastic. It's like he knows that within his circle people will actually listen to him.

I work in services and I know that no matter how well-intentioned we are about trying to empower a person, real improvement rarely happens. Planning meetings especially are seldom 'owned' by the person.

Another important difference is how Andrew and I are relating as brothers. I guess before we had a typical relationship in that Andrew would keep a lot of things close to his chest. He would often tell me to 'get lost' if I tried to talk with him about the future. Now I am helping him to facilitate the circle. We work very closely together. It's hard to describe, but we definitely relate differently when talking about his circle.

I believe Andrew's circle is for life, so that when perhaps family members are not around, Andrew has other people who will always make sure his best interests are listened to and acted on.

A circle is a brilliant way of involving ordinary people in a meaningful and mutual way; and supporting a person who has previously been isolated or restricted to realise their potential.

A comparison of three types of planning for people with disabilities

Traditional planning	Person-centred teams	Circles of support
Purpose of the planning meeting		
To co-ordinate services across different disciplines. To clarify staff roles in the implementation of training programmes.	To establish a common vision for all staff. To discover information needed to focus organisational change.	To establish and support a personal vision for an individual. To build community support and action on behalf of the focus person.
Composition of the team		
Professionals and specialists.	Professionals, direct service workers. May include focus person and family.	Focus person and his spokesperson, family, friends and associates. May include some human service workers.
Where does the team meet?		
Human service setting conference room: centralised site.	Human service setting close to direct service workers; group home, workshop: decentralised site.	Community setting: living room, church room, library meeting room. Places close to where members live.
How often does the group meet?		
Once a year with quarterly reviews.	Major investment in initial sessions. Quarterly or monthly reviews.	Typically, once a month with sub-meetings in-between as necessary for on-going problem-solving.
Who initiates the meeting and for what purpose?		
Team leader initiates to meet requirements of regulations.	Organisational change agent initiates to find new directions for the organisation.	Focus person or spokesperson initiates to reach goals they are unable to accomplish working alone.
What motivates people to attend the meeting?		
Avoidance of punishment by regulators. Interest in co-ordination of departmental units.	Interest in organisational innovation and finding new directions for focus person.	Voluntary commitment by people who are interested in helping someone they care for.
Nature of the images for the future		
Goals will fit within existing programme options.	Goals will reflect new programme models and options yet to be developed.	Vision will reflect desire of focus person and family

cont.

A comparison of three types of planning for people with disabilities *(cont.)*

Traditional planning	Person-centred teams	Circles of support
Roles of members and boundaries of action		
Members have specific roles and clear boundaries for action. Plans do not change roles or boundaries. Members act within formal existing organisational channels of authority.	Members' roles will change based on new directions. Old boundaries for action may be changed to allow for new action. Plans may change roles and create new agendas for action. Members create new channels and connections to accomplish their goals.	Participant roles are constantly changing based on tasks. Boundaries for action are defined by personal vision and commitment of group members. Members use informal networks and contacts to open doors in community.
Product of an effective group meeting		
Completed forms, paperwork. Specific goals to use to evaluate programme effectiveness.	An agenda for organisational change. A shared understanding of new directions for change.	Commitments to action by community members. Significant quality of life changes for the focus person.
Role of human service worker		
Set all direction. Organise all activity. Co-ordinate direct service worker activities.	Mediate interests of providers and focus person. Lead organisational change efforts. Listen to direct service workers.	Support directions defined by group. Increase knowledge of available resources. Provide direct services to focus person.
Role of community members		
Not involved in the process.	May help implement some ideas.	Generate and implement plan and action steps.
Role of person with a disability		
Comply with the plan.	Co-operate in the development of the plan.	Direct plan and activities.

Source: Mount B. *et al. What Are We Learning about Circles of Support? A collection of tools, ideas and reflections on building and facilitating circles of support.* Manchester (CT): Communities Inc, 1998.

Staffing

To achieve real inclusion all staff must work differently with community-building and relationships becoming central to their activities. Some services are also appointing staff specifically to develop inclusive opportunities; for example, community access officers or community bridge-builders. (See also Chapter 5, Getting a life, not a building). Such people share the following characteristics:

- Willingness to be a pioneer – a different voice – not afraid to be the only dissenter
- Stamina and commitment – a determination to make things work
- Enthusiasm – ability to engage with people and bring them on board
- Creativity and lateral thinking – doing things in unexpected ways
- Flexibility, patience and tolerance.

Community access officers

Cardiff Social Services appointed two full-time workers to develop opportunities for people to participate in community activities and contribute to local life. They work creatively, using their own initiative to open up new and different opportunities according to what individuals require. This can range from joining the local Ramblers Club to setting up a small craft business.

The community access officers' job is to facilitate new opportunities rather than work with individuals on a long-term basis. They spend time finding out what someone wants to do, then seek out the opportunity and arrange any necessary support. They have a small budget which is used only if necessary to pump-prime an activity – for example, if someone is getting involved in gardening they might buy some tools to start them off.

Focusing on the facilitation role enables them to work with a larger number of people and they can concentrate on finding new opportunities, making contacts and building networks, thus at the same time developing their own skills as effective community bridge-builders.

Managing risk

How to manage risk-taking is a recurring theme in discussions about inclusion. There are the risks from an individual simply going to and fro in the community. There are the risks associated with volunteer recruitment and the risks taken by staff while working to broaden people's experiences and help them learn new skills.

Men and women with learning difficulties must have the opportunity to understand risk and develop skills in handling it. This may simply mean strengthening and supporting the understanding of someone who can take good care of themselves already. Or it might mean arranging for someone to attend a personal-safety training course or a sex education course. Every person is different and degrees of risk should be measured according to the needs of each individual.

What sort of screening process should be used when introducing new people? There are no easy answers to this. On the one hand, people's experience of meeting new people must be as 'ordinary' as possible – how many of us only ever meet new people who have first gone through a screening process! – and on the other hand we must recognise that many of those we support are very vulnerable and appropriate safeguards need to be installed.

Police checks are used by some organisations but not by others. Should they be part of the volunteer recruitment process? They can be a good deterrent and they reassure parents and carers. Others feel they take up a lot of time and are not a guarantee. They give a false sense of security. In addition, the checking-up culture contradicts the aim of building friendships.

We need a process which takes account of the service's responsibility to safeguard the individual but which can still respond positively and creatively to their particular needs and wishes: an approach that involves getting to know each person very well. What support does this person need? Physical support – because of disability or health needs? Travel support – for instance, a person might say they know their way home, but do they really? It's about knowing the reality for each person.

It helps to:

- share responsibility and risk. For example, a worker can share concerns and agree action with another worker or concerned person
- put concerns in writing
- think carefully about why any procedure is being put in place. Is it genuine concern for the individual or only to 'cover our own backs' – in which case, would stronger support from managers be a better solution?

Services which have long lists of requirements, rules and regulations are not helping people to break out of the service culture and develop a more typical lifestyle.

Helping people stay local

SAWSTON IS AN ATTRACTIVE village about 12 miles from Cambridge. Around a dozen people with learning difficulties currently travel from Sawston and the surrounding area to day centres in Cambridge. These people are being helped to base their lives in and around their local community: to continue doing things they already enjoy and develop new opportunities in and around Sawston.

Sawston already has a number of advantages:

- The Compass Centre – a small day centre in an ordinary house which currently supports about 15 people with complex needs.
- A village college firmly committed to community involvement and to enabling access to all its facilities for everyone, including people with disabilities.
- Compass Point Cafe run by people with learning difficulties.
- The Huntingdon Trust – a charitable trust able to offer financial help to local projects.
- An enthusiastic staff group committed to inclusion principles.

A community social evening provided an opportunity to increase understanding and knowledge of the future plans to help people in Sawston and encourage local citizens to get involved.

The work in Sawston is demonstrating the benefits of developing partnerships between social services, the voluntary sector and other local resources. Cambridge Social Services aims to replicate the Sawston practice in other local areas. ■

CAMBRIDGE SOCIAL SERVICES runs two small day services for people with complex needs, from ordinary premises in the villages of Fulbourn and Bottisham. These locations have made it possible to help people take responsibility for work such as arranging the flowers in church and winning a contract to keep the village litter-free. ■

IN HEREFORDSHIRE PEOPLE are contributing positively to their local communities through schemes like:

- clearing paths for National Heritage
- making props for the local dramatic society
- removing the cricket pavilion
- maintaining and improving the railway station waiting room. ■

USING A GRANT OF £15,000 FROM the Bridge House Trust, London Mencap has employed four facilitators, working five hours a week, to develop circles for young people in South London. Within four months five circles were started. The facilitators' sole task is to develop the circles. Freed up from office and other organisational tasks, they can concentrate on building relationships and community links. ■

It might not catch on ... it's far too simple

Personal reflections on the job of a community access officer

We cannot continue to extol the importance of individual need while at the same time creating more and more largely segregated services. Services have been improving but they are still 'services' and let's not kid ourselves otherwise. Instead of saying to people, *'These are the services available, which one will you choose?'*, we should simply ask, *'What would you really like to do?'*.

We still complain, *'Where is the range of services for people to fit into?'*. The answer is, *'It's all out there – to a large degree'*. There are plenty of exciting opportunities. But it's not a service, it's called the city, town or village where we live. All the talent, skills and ingredients we need are out there. They are not day service staff or social workers. They are butchers, bakers and candlestick makers.

The starting point is to ask *one* person what he or she *really* wants to do. Then go and make it happen for that *one* person. 'This is simplistic,' I hear you cry. Where is the flowchart and evidence from the USA?

If someone expresses an interest in learning to make jewellery we often rush about looking for a class or we set up a new group. Six months later we end up with a segregated group meeting miles from people's homes, with perhaps just 5 per cent of the class having any interest in the subject.

Why not search out a jeweller running a small business in town and talk to him or her? Perhaps they could support someone for a few hours a week, working from a *real* shop or workshop, passing on skills. Perhaps the person can learn enough to sell their own work and earn some money. Perhaps we could buy a supply of stock in return. If the first jeweller says 'No' we go and ask another. Eventually one will say yes ... Who knows what the possibilities are until we get out there.

Simplistic? Perhaps, but it can be done. There are many problems to overcome, negotiation skills to learn, agreements to be drawn up ... but that is what we're paid for! Why are we still so incapable of thinking creatively and small, casting our nets far and wide in search of a real community presence in an effort to make one person's dream come true?

It may be fashionable – or the easy way out? – to blame government policy or management, staff shortages or cuts, but that is not the answer. It's about changing attitudes, a change of emphasis. It is *our* problem at grassroots level. We must begin to make serious connections with the engineers, chefs, and farm-workers. Because they *are* the community and have all the skills we need.

In a city in England, service-brokerage is up and running on a small scale. Some clients now have some control over their slice of the financial cake. In every case, the client chose to buy in a pair of helping hands to support them in accessing the facilities some of us already enjoy. In one case, the worker was used as a job coach, in another to teach golf, in another to assist with a rambling club outing – all in the heart of the community. No-one bought a 'service'!

cont.

'What will be the positive outcomes?' is often the key question in funding applications. (Can someone please define a positive outcome? Who decides what is positive?) Funding increasingly depends on people moving on. In reality, 'moving on' too often means moving from one service to another and back again. Is six consecutive years on a college course positive? Is this a classic case of professional self-preservation?

How can we change the service/model/box-and-cox syndrome? Take one worker, give them a phone, a small monthly budget and a monthly bus card, a desk and an old filing cabinet. This person's role is to be a facilitator – he or she provides no transport/taxi-service and does not participate regularly in hands-on sessions.

The worker will say to the client over a cup of tea, 'Now ... what would you really like to do?', and see what develops. Given time you'll have people running a business, getting paid for jobs they really enjoy, walking with the ramblers, playing golf and doing all the things we all enjoy in a natural network of support from their own community.

All I know for certain is that it works. The problem is it might not catch on because it's far too simple to organise.

Funding

Most of the significant work on inclusion is being done by voluntary organisations or by small projects within statutory organisations. Often these are single worker projects, relying on short-term, hand-to-mouth funding. People working in this area who feel relatively secure about their funding are still as rare as gold-dust. A constantly recurring theme is the lack of stable funding and the time spent battling for more money. The problem is worsened because funders want results in numerical terms rather than taking proper account of the positive results which emerge from the quality of relationships. Services are seen as expensive because the long-term benefits are numerically invisible.

Perhaps inclusion should be incorporated into contracts and evaluated. But how do we measure inclusion? Does inclusion fit the 'contract culture'? Do we satisfy the service system at the expense of ordinary life'? How do we satisfy the legitimate need for accountability to funders without turning relationship- and community-building into a mechanical exercise?

These and other questions posed in this chapter remain a challenge for everyone committed to full inclusion for men and women with learning difficulties. A few services and a growing number of individual workers are showing the way. Much more needs to be done to get the majority moving in the same direction.

References

1. Amado A, Conklin F, Wells J. *Friends: A manual for connecting persons with disabilities and community members.* St Paul (Minnesota): Human Services Research and Development Center, 1990.

2. O'Brien J, Lyle O'Brien C. *Members of Each Other.* Canada: Inclusion Press, 1997.

Further reading

Wertheimer A. *Citizen Advocacy: A powerful partnership* (new edition). London: CAIT, 1998.

Williams M. Is it inclusion ... or just an illusion? *Llais* 1998; Winter, 47

Williams P. *Standing by Me: Stories of citizen advocacy.* London: CAIT, 1998.

Chapter 7

Planning for individuals

Vision and Principles

Understanding someone's aspirations cannot be achieved by functional assessments or using checklists. It can only come about through sustained intense personal contact, friendship and understanding – and a willingness to make informed guesses, accepting that we still get it wrong at times. (Changing Days, 1996)

Developing a service to match the unique requirements of each person is at the heart of this work. It is the bedrock on which services should be built. We must transform a service which expects people to fit into a limited number of activities to one which evolves a range of choices from what individuals say they want to do or would like to try.

There are a number of ways of planning with individual people, which include 'whole life' planning, personal futures planning, essential lifestyle planning and PATH. Whatever method is adopted, it is essential to look at the whole person rather than viewing them as merely a series of 'needs' – such as for residential, day or leisure services. Most importantly, this includes friendships and relationships, which are still not receiving enough emphasis. (See Chapter 5)

Person-centred planning is discussed in detail in *Changing Days*. In summary, the basic principles underlying the process are:

- ensure the individual is central
- involve the person's personal network
- focus on strengths and capacities
- create a vision for the future
- develop a personal profile
- start with achievable short-term goals
- keep things under review.

The ways in which services need to change to become truly person-centred are discussed in other chapters. Here we concentrate on the essential first step, a profiling process which captures the hopes, dreams and abilities of each individual. ■

The challenge of person-centred work in a system-centred world

Planning for individuals is not a new idea. Many organisations claim they base their services on individual needs. There is talk of 'individualising' services, but all too often this means people living in smaller groups but still segregated and still spending their days with other people who have learning disabilities. (*Changing Days,* 1996). Unfortunately, it is still unusual to find a service which has successfully moved away from a situation where professionals plan for groups of people to fit into existing frameworks to one which is built on a person-centred approach, catering for the individual needs of each man or woman with learning difficulties. Why does this appear to be so difficult?

The demands of the system often speak louder than the people it serves. Workers please bosses, mission statements, rules and regulations and funders. Goals in the service plan seem to relate more to the needs of the service than to the hopes and dreams of the men and women actually using it. They are passive recipients of the planning process rather than active participants in a life that belongs to them.

The system seems to offer perfection, order and rationality. If we just finish the paperwork, meet the deadlines, fill the quotas, then things will get better. But real life is not like that – it is often imperfect, uncertain, full of change, and for some people filled with chaos and disorder. Finding and building welcoming places in community life can be really hard work. It may be easier to turn to systems for some sense of security in the face of so much uncertainty in our world, our towns and neighbourhoods.

Person-centred work challenges existing organisations, professional roles and personal lifestyles. It challenges workers to push back against the demands of the system to have the time, energy and heart available to respond to people.[1]

Creating the profile

Everyone who knows the person well should be involved in the profiling/assessment process. This seems obvious but by no means always happens. Experience in the Changing Days sites showed that meeting to create a personal profile sometimes proved to be the first time day and residential staff had really sat down together for a proper conversation with an individual. Expressions such as, *'Oh, that explains why he says ...'* or *'Now that I know she can do that, we could try ...'* are common.

Sharing not only increases the pool of knowledge about somebody but also releases creativity and imagination about how to realise that person's dreams and ambitions.

It strengthens mutual support in his or her current network and can open doors to widening that network.

Making time for people to get together can be difficult and staff need support to treat this as a priority. Staff rotas and routines may need to be adjusted.

Front-line staff who support the person on a regular basis hold much information which it is vital to record, particularly in times of major service changes.

Small details as well as large should be recorded, particularly for people who can't easily communicate their needs. 'Getting up' and 'going to bed' routines are obvious examples, but what about things like: does he like to face towards light or away from it? Does she like to be fed a mouthful of meat before the vegetables or the other way round, or both together? How does he indicate 'yes' and 'no'?

Recording this information is important for a number of reasons:

* it ensures more consistency for the person
* it helps staff to work consistently: across shifts, between home and day care
* it becomes easier to get to know the person quicker: new staff, a new friend, agency staff
* it will be particularly important for people from minority ethnic backgrounds whose cultural needs may not be familiar to all staff working with them
* it helps ensure information doesn't get lost or forgotten as when a member of staff moves on to another job
* it is a valuable way of recording change and development in the person.

Make a life history book and include as much detail as possible about the person's past. This can help you understand what makes them tick and may reveal past interests or skills lost or forgotten through changed circumstances. A lady who lived at home into adulthood was used to carrying out many home-based tasks, such as cooking, ironing and washing. When her mother died she was put into an institution and lost all these skills. They were only rediscovered when she moved out into an ordinary house in the community.

Rules on confidentiality may need to be reconsidered. It has been disappointing to hear about access to notes often being denied on grounds which seem to have nothing to do with helping to build a profile of the person, but everything to do with maintaining bureaucratic rules and regulations – the 'we've always done it this way' syndrome.

The profile should be in a form that the person themselves can understand: use pictures, photographs, tapes and videos. It should be owned by them and wherever possible looked after by them: if not all of it, then at least parts of it, with support if necessary. This does not preclude the profile also containing all the written material for detailed planning and ensurance of the person's health and safety. Loose-leaf format allows sections to be included or removed where confidentiality is an issue or according to the person's preference.

The profile should be the first step in developing the person's community care assessment. There is still too much duplication of information gathering. Often two or three different departments or agencies are collecting the same information about the person but not linking with each other. Unfortunately, it happens too often that information gathered second-hand or by someone who has met the subject only briefly, if at all, is what actually determines the service that person receives.

The profile should be closely linked to the process which governs service planning. This is an important way of enabling an individual to influence decisions at the planning level.

Lessons learnt

All five changing days sites have been working to put individuals' needs first. In Hackney, extensive consultation about what people would like to do along with an individual profile of each person has been translated into Project Teams, each of which focuses on a particular area of activities and opportunities – Performing Arts, Sports, Fitness and Outdoor Pursuits, Homes and Gardens, Food and Drink, Creative Arts and Me and My Life. People are linked into different teams according to what they want to do. Instead of being connected to a day centre, people are connected to their interests. (See Chapter 3.)

Ely Hospital has developed a profile of each resident. A planning circle, made up of people who know the resident well, uses the information from the profile to arrange opportunities for people to begin trying new activities before they leave hospital. When they move out, instead of going to a day centre each person has an individualised programme based on being in the community and using ordinary services. (See Chapter 16.)

Contrasting assumptions and practices of system-centred and person-centred development

System-centred	Person-centred
Production and efficiency are the most important outcomes	Quality of life is the most important outcome
Subordinates needs of people to the maintenance of bureaucracy	Subordinates needs of service system to the needs and interests of people
People are seen as objects to be processed by the system	People are critical actors with deep desires who shape their own future
People's interests are often ignored, sometimes exploited	Human growth and dignity in the process of change are critical
Control for decisions is allocated to professionals who know best	Control for decisions is placed in the hands of the people
Complex regulations and procedures sustain professional interests	Quality of support depends on good information and creativity
Detachment is the preferred stance with people	Workers develop personal relationships with people
Direct line workers are often devalued, ignored or exploited	Direct line workers are equally valued as critical actors
Service designs are standardised and dictated by centralised authorities	Service designs are highly diverse and come from people in their communities
Workers rely on legal charters, formal authority and control structures to motivate action	Workers rely on family, neighbourhood, community organisations and associations to provide social support and stability
Resources are allocated to increase the holdings of services and the benefits of professionals	Resources are invested in supports that help people be more effective at meeting needs for themselves
Offers the promise of perfection at the expense of the diversity of the people and the workers	Offers the richness of imperfection at the expense of order and control

Source: Adapted from Korean D. *People-Centred Development: Toward a framework.*
West Hartford (CT): Kumarian Press, 1984.

Multi-media profiling

ACTING UP IS PART OF THE Matchbox Theatre Trust which since 1986 has been working with people who are marginalised by severe communication difficulties and institutional attitudes. Acting Up believes that no matter how difficult it may be for some individuals, everyone can communicate. Their aim has been to demonstrate that people with severe learning disabilities have a lot to say about their lives. By using information from the past and present in the form of still and moving images and with the help of a touch screen, people with high support needs and very little verbal communication can own this material, share it and help plan their future.

A portfolio of photographs, sound and video clips is put onto a computer – signs for yes and no, cues for pleasure and pain, their life story, details about their family and friends, and any other important information.

This method of profiling empowers a person and engages them from the beginning. It can be used alongside the community care assessment and can be a powerful tool for collecting information and informing individual care plans. The profile is available on computer and/or video and the person themselves can share the information with key workers or new staff.

When it comes to case conferences, people using services don't just attend, they present themselves. They interact and involve others in a living account of themselves and their past. The service user is clearly centre stage, which is where he or she should be. ■

✓ Checklist

Does the profile provide:

- ◆ information in a form that can be accessed by the user?
- ◆ a structured starting point for a new or changed relationship?
- ◆ a more equal relationship based on respect through shared experience?
- ◆ a lasting resource that is regularly updated, kept active and effective?
- ◆ a detailed and engaging picture of the service user?
- ◆ strong, clear statements of a person's needs and abilities?
- ◆ evidence of the individual way a person communicates?

Contact: John Ladle, Acting Up, 90 De Beauvoir Road, London N1 4EN. Tel: 0171 275 9173

Reference

1. Mount B. *Imperfect Change: Embracing the tensions of person-centred work.* Manchester (CT): Communitas, 1990.

Further reading

Azmi S *et al.* Listening to adolescents and adults with intellectual disabilities from South Asia communities. *Journal of Applied Research in Intellectual Disabilities* 1997; 10(3): 250–63

Hussain F. Life story work for people with learning disabilities. *British Journal of Learning Disabilities* 1997; Vol. 25.

Refer to Chapter 7 of *Changing Days* for list of useful reading.

Chapter 8

Keeping users central – the collective voice

Vision and Principles

Genuine partnership with and involvement of users is critical if new daytime opportunities are to be truly person-centred and reflect the needs and aspirations of users, their families and friends.
(Changing Days, 1996)

Achieving effective partnership with men and women with learning difficulties requires a change in the service culture so that it is seen as everyone's responsibility.

Commitment to user involvement must be evident in policy and practice from top to bottom of the organisation:

- written – in policy and procedure documents, such as recruitment of staff
  - in guidelines setting out rights and responsibilities on both sides (staff and users)
  - included in job descriptions at all levels
- verbal – a culture where users are valued as partners, spoken about and respected as individuals with gifts to offer; where everyone working in the organisation accepts and acknowledges the inclusion of users and where many staff, not necessarily directly working in disability services, know personally someone who uses the service.

In a well-run service, resources for user involvement are part of mainstream funding, not just an add-on offered when there is some spare money, or reliant only on short-term or external funding. Staff time is allocated to it so that it does not have to depend on individual, committed staff who support it in their own time.

Opportunities for staff and users to train together should be an integral part of the training strategy.

Policy and practice should extend across agencies, particularly day and residential services, so that good practice is consistent through all areas of people's lives. ■

What would an effective user involvement strategy look like?

In a service with effective user involvement we would see:

Strategic level

- Regular contact with users by people at the top:
  - users attending council meetings
  - councillors attending user meetings
  - planners and policy-makers attending user meetings
  - managers meeting with user representatives regularly (e.g. three-monthly to hear and act on concerns rising from grassroots)
- Users on committees and sub-groups with appropriate support
- Parallel user groups with negotiating power and a clear process for joint working with staff/professional groups
- A budget for user involvement seen as essential and non-negotiable. Hackney has appointed a user involvement officer as part of the reorganisation of services. In Hereford, social services funded five extra hours a week for the current independent facilitator to support user involvement in day services development
- Users involved in monitoring and evaluation; including taking the lead on evaluating, as described in *Looking at Our Services*[1]
  - an ongoing monitoring and updating process (particularly to ensure inclusion of people with complex needs)
  - one-off, short-term evaluation exercises
- User involvement written into contracts. Providers should be able to demonstrate how they enable the collective voice of users to be heard and give examples of how users influence the way their service operates

Practice level

- Users centrally involved in all aspects of planning about their lives
- Users choosing their own support workers with a move towards hiring and managing their own workers with help from direct payments legislation
- An effective person-centred planning procedure which ensures that users' views are heard by planners
- Easy-to-use and well-used complaints procedure
- Active user groups and committees in homes, day centres and clubs, which can demonstrate that users are sharing power and control with professionals
- User groups specifically for people from minority ethnic groups to provide

opportunities to meet people from their own culture, speak their own language and discuss issues of particular relevance to their cultural group

- A user involvement officer – preferably an independent person, perhaps linked to an advocacy scheme – appointed to promote and support user involvement across the service
- A member of staff in each facility whose job is to spend at least part of their time supporting users specifically in collective voice activities. Don't rely on the user involvement officer to do everything. For example, people need support not only to get to meetings and take part in them but support later when they report back to their peers and staff
- Joint training as a regular practice: – users and staff training together
  – users training staff
- Users involved in the appointment of staff, formally as well as informally
- Users working in health, social services and education offices (paid, unpaid, full time, part time) would be a familiar sight. All offices would have a proactive policy towards this end
- User-friendly, accessible information in different languages and formats
- Advocacy services

Progress

Three Changing Days user groups were established, in Cambridge, Hackney and Hereford, to work parallel to but linking with the professional steering groups. All have resulted in increased self-confidence and skills for individuals, enjoyment in meeting and getting to know people, and a strengthened collective user voice locally.

The groups had three major aims:

- to increase people's knowledge and experience of opportunities – day, evening and weekends – for people in the community
- to develop ways in which users could be involved in working for change in day services
- to strengthen the voice of users locally and increase their influence and involvement with the planning and delivery of services.

All three areas already had various means by which people could speak up – student committees, house groups, self-advocacy groups – but the Changing Days groups were the first time that they had got together on a representative basis. To represent a wide cross-section of views, life experiences and hopes and dreams, they made sure to include people from different living situations – those living independently, those in group homes, and those with family – and different day activities, such as in work, going to a day centre or going to college.

Achievements of these groups included:

- taking part in Changing Days steering groups alongside professionals. This has involved slowing the pace of meetings, producing minutes and other material in accessible formats and providing support for people before, during and after meetings.
- speaking to social services committee members about their ideas for future day services.
- working with professionals to develop a policy on the involvement of users in staff recruitment.
- visiting different parts of their own and other people's services. Users often don't know what choices and opportunities exist within their own local services. They don't visit other parts of the service to see people in work-related jobs, for example. Visits to services further afield help people learn about different opportunities and also to make comparisons with their current services.
- making videos of their lives and services.
- searching out new opportunities locally – places to go, things to do.
- taking photographs to help people identify new staff and their new roles in services.
- creating a booklet about how to make friends and about things to do in the community which cost little or nothing.[2]

The development of the groups has been achieved through:

- strong, consistent support from committed staff, often over and above the call of duty
- verbal, written and financial support from management
- pictorial versions of documents about changes in services
- managers maintaining direct and regular contact with users
- willingness to adapt meeting times, places and structures.

In Belfast and Cardiff, users have been involved more as individuals than in groups. In Belfast, users played a large part in organising a two-day event held at the beginning of the Changing Days work, which included exhibitions of their current work and lives. A small group at a day centre worked on their individual profiles and were involved in various meetings. People living in Ely Hospital have been involved through Ely People First.

References

1. Whittaker A. *Looking at Our Services – service evaluation by people with learning difficulties.* London. King's Fund, 1996.

2. *The Talkabout Book: Friends.* Contact: Jenni Morgan, Hereford Citizen Advocacy, Community House, 25 Castle Street, Hereford HR1 2NW. Tel: 01432 263757.

Further reading

Beresford P. A profitable venture? *Community Care* 1997; 29 May.

Lewis J. *Give Us a Voice: Towards equality for Black and minority ethnic people with learning difficulties.* London: Choice Press, 1996.

Lindow V. *Community Service Users as Consultants and Trainers.* Leeds: Department of Health, 1996.

Morris J. *Encouraging User Involvement in Commissioning: A resource for commissioners.* Leeds: Department of Health, 1996.

National User and Carer Group. *Consultation Counts: Guidelines for service purchasers and users and carers.* Leeds: Department of Health, 1996.

Norah Fry Research Centre. *Plain Facts.* Issue No.3: Making Complaints. Issue No.7: Choosing Staff. Bristol: Norah Fry Research Centre, 1996.

Redworth M, Philips G. Involving people with learning disabilities in community care planning. *British Journal of Learning Disabilities* 1997; 25:31–5

Ross K. Speaking in tongues: involving users in day care services. *British Journal of Social Work* 1995; 25:791–804

The User-Centred Services Group. *Building Bridges between People Who Use and People Who Provide Services.* London: National Institute for Social Work, 1993.

Townsley R, Howarth J, Le Grys P, Macadam M. *Getting Involved in Choosing Staff: A resource pack for supporters, trainers and staff working with people with learning difficulties.* Brighton: Pavilion Publishing.

Chapter 9

Involving parents and families

Vision and Principles

> *Genuine partnership with and involvement of users and carers is critical if new daytime opportunities are to be truly person-centred and reflect the needs and aspirations of users, their families and friends.* (Changing Days, 1996)

Creating a partnership with parents and other family carers from the outset is essential. When parents feel they are working with the services as trusted partners, real progress is much more likely.

Partnership means developing a strategy which is grounded in active involvement, is on-going, has commitment from parents and professionals, has a framework or timetable which keeps the process on track and where everyone shares in the aims and can see the outcomes.

Parents' stories of change are very influential in helping other parents accept change and many will be willing to use their own community links to find new opportunities for people.

Many parents are looking for change and welcome new opportunities. But this must go hand in hand with careful planning and a balancing of their wishes with the needs of their sons and daughters. ■

What parents look for from services

Evolution vs revolution

Many parents are suspicious and fearful of revolutionary changes in services and would prefer an evolutionary approach – slow and cautious – with careful preparation and planning. Many will have fought to get the current service and even if not entirely happy with it, will be fearful of losing it. They may need a lot of convincing that the proposed changes are based on a genuine desire to improve people's lives and are not just another cost-cutting exercise.

This may conflict with the service's desire to speed things up and avoid running two types of service at the same time. A balance must be struck between going so slowly that nothing really changes and going so fast that it alienates everyone.

Reliability and consistency

When you are used to seeing your son or daughter safely off by minibus to the day centre each morning before setting off for work yourself, it can be a major cause of anxiety and upheaval if that pattern changes and they start going to different places, at different times and on different days.

Although many parents will agree that large, segregated buildings are not ideal, they will not readily accept closure of the day centre, particularly if their sons or daughters have complex needs. They will be looking for assurance that there will still be a secure and practical base – even if it is a small one.

They will want to know where everyone is and what they are doing. Will there be a central telephone for contacts? What happens if people get lost? What back-up plans are there? An important part of the new service will be a risk-taking policy which reassures parents but which is flexible enough to allow people to try new experiences and learn new skills.

Level of service

When major changes are proposed, parents may need a guarantee that an equivalent level of service will be provided. Others will be prepared to accept a bit less in quantity if they are assured of significantly higher quality.

There may be conflicts between parents' needs and users' needs. For example, if a young man is taken to football on a Saturday afternoon, will one of his parents have to take a half-day off work during the week?

Experience shows that parents who at first are fiercely opposed to any reduction in hours often end up working with services more flexibly because they see how much the new-style service is benefiting their son or daughter.

A parent who was initially opposed to his daughter changing her daily routine of attending the day centre on the minibus was later prepared to share the cost of a taxi when he realised how much she was gaining through new opportunities and life choices.

Communication

When parents talk about being involved in service changes, effective communication comes high on their list of priorities. However, there is no perfect formula and no-one gets it entirely right. But services must devote time and resources to plan for communicating with all stakeholders. This is particularly important at the beginning, but must continue through the period of change and afterwards. Hackney Social Services spent a year in the first phase of involving people – gathering ideas on current and future services, arranging visits to other services and consulting organisations and individuals – before producing the first document that outlined their proposals. After a further four months, a five year plan was produced.

Communicating with parents of people with complex needs

Many parents will agree that the needs of their sons and daughters are different from their own and are often not known or best met by parents and carers. Nevertheless, particularly in times of change, it is important that parents of people with complex needs are kept regularly informed. In new-style services, people will be moving around from place to place much more during the day, there will be a lot of new activities going on and new or different staff will be working with their sons and daughters.

Parents need regular, perhaps daily, news about how their sons or daughters are getting on. For example, a simple notebook diary which can be carried round with the person and in which staff write a few words about what they've been doing and how they have responded to it. Parents otherwise get no feedback. Lack of news creates anxiety and does not allow parents to share fully in the new opportunities, progress and enjoyment of new skills and activities.

Staff may object that it will take too much time but this small amount of effort is important in creating closer partnership and mutual understanding.

'Consult us at the beginning – not after you've done three drafts of your plans!'
'Listen to us'
'Be honest'
'Communicate regularly with us'

Carers (Recognition and Services) Act 1995

The Carers (Recognition and Services) Act 1995 is consistent with the Government's policy aims for both community care and disabled children – 'to *ensure that service providers make practical support for carers a high priority'* and that *'assessment of care needs should always take account of the needs of caring family, friends and neighbours'*. The Act is concerned with carers who are either providing or intending to provide a substantial amount of care on a regular basis. Under the Act, a carer is entitled, on request, to an assessment when a local authority carries out an assessment of the person cared for in respect of community care services or services for children. The result of the carer's assessment should be taken into account when the local authority is making decisions about services to be provided to the user.

Carers (Recognition and Services) Act 1995: Policy Guidance
Carers (Recognition and Services) Act 1995: Practice Guide

Copies free of charge from: Department of Health, PO Box 410, Wetherby LS23 7LN.
Fax: 01937 845381

✓ Checklist for managers

Senior managers must keep in touch with the needs of individuals. They must be sensitive to parents' fears, anxieties and expectations. They need to know the local history of services to understand the personal backgrounds involved and to appreciate the differences in experience and expectations of services that exist between younger and older people.

Communication
◆ Communicate regularly with parents – not just when there is major news.

cont.

◆ A newsletter can provide regular information, updates on progress, a letters page for exchange of questions, ideas and worries, stories of change in people's lives, examples of services in other areas. Parents and people with learning difficulties can be involved in producing it.

◆ Use the post! Seems obvious, but as one parent said: 'If you just send notes or letters on the coach, I often don't get them.'

◆ No jargon! Clear, simple ordinary language will benefit everyone. For example, 'focus group' may be a familiar term in services but does it help the lay-person? Better to choose a name which describes what the group is: 'new ideas', 'transport'. Avoid ambiguity: one group of parents got the impression from an early draft planning document that all centres were closing when in fact they were not. Be sensitive about wording. ;Users are telling us ...' may not ring true to parents of people with complex needs who feel their son or daughter is incapable of 'telling' staff.

◆ Produce material in whatever languages are needed for people from minority ethnic groups in your area.

◆ Give as much nuts and bolts information as possible. For example, when writing consultative documents, include ideas about options for the future. With the best of intentions, managers may try not to be too specific about future plans in order to be open to everyone's ideas and to avoid the accusation that 'you've decided already'. However, if no concrete suggestions are made, parents may fill the vacuum with the worst-case scenario, particularly those with bad experiences. As one parent said: 'We are so used to thinking in one direction it is hard to imagine a different way.'

Meetings

◆ Use a variety of opportunities for people to get together – parents, users and staff.

◆ Large meetings have their purpose – particularly at the beginning when you are gathering ideas and views and want to make sure everyone is involved. But large meetings are often dominated by confident, outspoken speakers who may be positive or negative towards new ideas. Either way, it can be difficult to get an accurate idea of how most people are feeling.

◆ On the whole, small meetings work better. It is easier to ensure that everyone has a chance to contribute their views and can talk through issues in detail to reach clearer understanding.

◆ Provide opportunities for one-to-one meetings. Some parents will prefer this to group discussion. People need opportunities to contribute ideas privately and it is important to set aside time to allow this individual approach.

◆ There must be a clearly understood process by which parents can be sure their views reach decision-makers.

cont.

◆ Arrange meetings at different times of the day and evening according to the requirements of parents. Announce them well in advance so parents can plan ahead. Provide sit-in support to encourage meeting attendance.

◆ Provide opportunities for parents and staff to meet socially away from service settings. This is a valuable way to break down barriers and build trust between parents and staff at all levels.

◆ If parents only meet service people when there is a problem this fosters perceptions that parents are 'difficult' or 'obstructive'. When parents and professionals have the opportunity to meet on other occasions, each side often finds they have a surprising amount in common! Social functions are another way to hear success stories and celebrate.

◆ Arrange opportunities for parents to visit other services.

◆ Explore specific areas where parents might help. For example, in Havering, a parent with wide experience of transport issues, headed the sub-group examining ways to create a more flexible transport system for the new service.

Partners in policy-making

PARTNERS IN POLICY-MAKING is a comprehensive leadership programme designed to achieve policy and systems change involving disabled people and their parents. The programme is underpinned by a strong values base of inclusion and disability equality. It covers:

- History of the disability movement and parent empowerment
- Education
- Whole life planning
- Employment
- Policy development – laws about service provision and how to influence them

- Assistive technology
- Supported living
- Advocacy – learning the skills: e.g. meeting officials, using the media, community organising, public speaking
- Community inclusion

Further information from: Circles Network, Pamwell House, 160 Pennywell Road, Upper Easton, Bristol BS5 0TX. Tel: 0117 939 3917; Fax: 0117 939 3918

Further reading

Azmi S *et al. Improving Services for Asian People with Learning Disabilities: The views of users and carers.* Manchester: Adrian Research Centre, 1996

Partnerships in Practice – the experience of South and East Belfast Trust

Effective partnerships take time to develop. They need high levels of commitment, good humour and clarity of purpose from those involved if they are to work. Working in partnership is tough, challenging, at times uncertain, sometimes messy and frequently uncomfortable (especially at the start).

It is no exaggeration to say that without the commitment of a small group of able, enthusiastic, far-sighted and courageous parents, prepared to work tirelessly in partnership with professionals over many years, the developments of the past decade in South and East Belfast Trust would simply not have happened.

Tackling a need

In the early 1970s, parents and people with learning difficulties in Belfast had little to look forward to. Services were few and far between and those that did exist were usually run in old buildings with few amenities. By the early 1980s things had improved a little. A new day centre was opened, there were hostels to provide alternative accommodation and increasing numbers of social workers and nurses in the community.

Though pleased with progress, a number of parents wanted more for their sons and daughters – education, training, work opportunities, travel, friends, fun – basically the same things as their brothers and sisters enjoyed.

At the time much of this seemed an impossible dream, but the parents were determined and, along with a number of equally committed professionals, formed the Orchardville Society in 1984. Fourteen years later, while not all of the dreams have yet been realised, very significant changes have happened, not least in how the relationship between parents and professionals has developed.

Developments have included 'on-site' job-sampling and training in a variety of work settings; the Orchardville Business Centre; the Edgcumbe Cafe, a bottle sorting business, and Project Career (a European funded project aimed at providing career education and progression).

They are now exploring how people with more complex needs can be included in training and social opportunities; how supported employment can be expanded and are developing 'circles of friends'.

The Society has also arranged joint visits for parents and health and social services staff to learn more about innovative practice across Europe and along with the local health and social service trust has played a key role in the development of inter-agency working in South and East Belfast over the past five years.

cont.

A truly collaborative approach

From the start it was essential to parents that staff 'on the ground' and senior managers acknowledged their concerns about the risks involved in stepping out into the unknown and in developing new services. A climate had to be created in which trust could develop. This required:

◆ *Strong leadership from the top* i.e. senior managers in health and social services and other agencies openly acknowledging, through their actions, that they recognised and valued the contribution parents could make to help change their children's future; parents choosing respected leaders who were able to represent their cause and who were willing to give up precious free time to work alongside service givers to bring about change.

◆ Parents and service providers *recognising and jointly managing risk* by:

  – acknowledging individuals' health and safety needs and planning around these;

  – using able and trusted staff to set up new projects;

  – health and social services agreeing to underwrite calculated financial risks in new projects (although this was rarely, if ever, called upon);

  – health and social services maintaining a safety net for people to return to if an alternative placement did not work.

◆ Leaders *spending time, listening, talking, learning, understanding* each other's respective pressures and constraints, and then agreeing realistic steps for making progress.

◆ People being open to learning and as knowledge increased, being willing to change their attitude.

◆ Parents and service providers *recognising* each other's *boundaries* i.e. clarifying what was expected of each partner before projects started, for experience showed that unless roles and responsibilities were clear in the beginning, the potential for misunderstanding and unnecessary conflict was considerable.

◆ People being *honest and open*, willing to admit mistakes and recognise service shortcomings.

◆ People *taking time to laugh, grieve, celebrate and learn* together and knowing each other well enough to do so.

◆ Parents and service providers having the *courage* and *insight* to *let go* and *move on* when the time was right.

◆ Parents and service givers *continuing to dream* and strive together to find new ways of making these dreams come true (joint visits to see other services were particularly helpful).

Contact: Hugh Connor, Head of Adult Services, South and East Belfast Trust, Knockbracken Healthcare Park, Saintfield Road, Belfast BT8 8HB. Tel: 01232 565 555 Fax: 01232 565 813

Chapter 10

Transition – moving towards adulthood

Vision and Principles

Transition is about change and 'new beginnings'. It should induce anticipation and excitement but also a healthy dose of anxiety because it is a venture into the unknown. The changes that occur naturally as we move from childhood through adolescence and into adulthood are full of confusion. We can't wait to be grown up but we also want to hang on to what we know and feel uncertain about the future.

Service transition can cover moves to further education, vocational and residential placements. A range of other issues that may also affect the transition period are family circumstances, the skills of the young adult and general planning for the future. Transition is not only a time of change for the young person but also for their family. The usual patterns of involvement of parents in the young person's life will change. At a time when critical decisions have to be made, a range of new professionals and agencies has to be introduced.[1]

Parents and family members play an essential part in this successful transition. They need clear information and must be prepared to ask questions and challenge the system. Parents whose sons and daughters have already left school will be an important source of knowledge.

Social workers, care managers and other professionals must ensure that both assessment and planning are organised effectively. Good advance planning gives everyone the chance to be prepared and promotes confidence in the process.

Spend time with the young person so that they feel valued as an individual. They should be at the centre of the planning process and actively involved in all decisions. Meetings to plan transition should not be held without them. All information available to the professional participants should also be given in a comprehensible form to the young people. ■

Two stories

When Beth was coming up to school-leaving age, I was really worried. As a single parent I felt very responsible for getting it right. The social worker called and explained that an assessment of Beth's needs would be necessary. We all got together, including Beth, with a teacher from school and talked about the things she liked to do, what she was good at and where she needed help. I was pleased – it felt that people were really interested in her.

'Beth now has a full week of activities which she enjoys and we meet every six months to see how things are progressing. She would like to attend the local college with her friend and we are looking for a volunteer to support her with the travelling. It's amazing – I never imagined I would have the confidence to consider these things were possible. We have all worked very well together.

This is one parent's positive experience and will set the scene for her daughter to progress to an even better future. But the reality for many young people with learning disabilities and their parents is very different. The move from the security of school into the world of adult services is one fraught with anxiety and perhaps conflict with the agencies who provide those services. For every positive story there are many others which describe ineffective and inefficient service systems; a lack of co-operation within and between statutory agencies; failure to give comprehensive and accurate information and an apparent unwillingness to respond flexibly to the needs of individuals.

When our son Michael was approaching school-leaving age we knew he should have an assessment – the school had told us. Three separate dates were planned and then cancelled because one or other of the professionals could not make it. I had planned to take time off work and we had tried to explain to our son what would be happening. It was all a waste of time and effort. After I became angry a meeting did go ahead. It was like talking to strangers. Apart from the school staff no-one there really knew Michael and we had to tell our story for the umpteenth time. Michael needs a lot of support and sometimes you just get too tired to put up with it.

School has often been a 'security blanket' for parents and young people alike. Moving away from that security can be difficult, especially if the future feels uncertain. For professionals, the leaving school assessment is often the first occasion when they have had to confront the tensions that can exist between the parents' need for a settled future and their child's hopes and dreams for adult life.

Being prepared

Young people with learning difficulties need the chance to inform themselves by 'doing'. Written material can only convey limited information and is frequently inaccessible anyway. Support will clearly be needed for young people who find it difficult to create opportunities for themselves.

They need to talk to family and friends about things they enjoy doing and things they would like to try. They need to talk to family and friends about college and work to get to know what it is like to be a student or an employee. Visits to workplaces and colleges will help people discover what is on offer and what suits them best.

Young people need to learn about being an adult and the responsibilities of citizenship if they are to play a meaningful part in the life of their community and in wider society.

These are critical elements of the latter stages of school life if all concerned are to approach the change to adulthood with confidence.

The importance of information

Information is useful only if it is clear, accurate and available at the right time. Families frequently complain that they have little or no information or they spend a lot of time wading through masses of written material only to find much of it irrelevant.

Information must be accessible to all people to whom it is relevant. It is still unusual to find information translated into other languages, so much depends on the ability to read and speak English. Terminology and concepts may need careful translating. For example, some cultures do not have a term to cover 'respite'. It is important to have workers from the same cultural group as parents.

What information should be available?

- A statement of rights for people who use services, and for their parents, relatives and carers
- An explanation of services available, what they offer, what needs they can meet, the costs and the catchment area
- Details of benefits and financial help
- Written standards and agreements related to each area of service
- Sources of self help from other people with similar experiences
- How to make comments, suggestions or complaints including access to advocacy or representation

How should it be made available?

- Be certain that the information is circulated in a way that ensures it will reach the people for whom it is intended

- Present information in clear language and avoid jargon

- Where technical terms have to be used, explain what they mean

- Publish it in the main community languages, and be prepared to translate it into the less common ones

- Use a variety of media formats, such as audio tape, video and so on

- Remember word of mouth – it is essential that professionals are well informed about all aspects of their services, as well as other services, and telling them in person is often the best way

- At the right time – people can benefit from information only if they get it when they need it

- Ensure that information comes from the right person – sometimes young people and their families will accept information from others with similar experiences with more confidence than if they hear it from professionals

'A Partnership in Caring' Max Wide
Contact: United Response, 113 Upper Richmond Road, London SW15 2TL

Finally, but perhaps most importantly of all, ensure that everyone knows it is okay to dream, to aspire to something new. Many services have proved that they can be amazingly creative and responsive to individual needs. Don't just accept second best.

Listen to people with learning disabilities

'If people with learning disabilities are to achieve the lifestyle they desire, we need to understand from their viewpoint ... For some people these preferences have already been expressed many times but the service system had no way of being able to listen or respond to what was being said. For others, years of not being listened to has had the effect of silencing their expression of choice.' Listening to People. National Development Team – consultation exercise with people with learning disabilities in Essex, February 1997

If there was ever an important time to be listened to, it is the time when a young person moves from adolescence into the adult world. The dignity and respect shown to a young man's or woman's sense of themselves at this point in their lives is critical to their sense of confidence about future opportunities.

Recognise that families are for life!

Helping a person with learning disabilities plan for their adult future can pose real dilemmas for professional staff. In recognising the individuality and adulthood of the young person, by listening and responding to their hopes and dreams, there may be real conflict with the perception of parents of their son's or daughter's needs. Parents may end up feeling totally excluded and the young person caught between uncompromising sides.

Parents can, of course, accept that their role with their son or daughter will change over time, particularly as new adult relationships develop – friends, partners, work colleagues. The anxiety for parents in these instances is often that these new relationships will not develop and that they themselves will remain the only enduring supporters.

It is crucial that parents are enabled to feel a sense of real partnership with their sons or daughters as well as with professionals as the process of planning for the future begins. No amount of expertise can replace the unique experience and knowledge of family members.

Families are for life – they will be offering support long after the professionals are gone. In order to build effective partnerships that benefit young people there must be open and honest consultation which values all contributions: real participation, not token consultation after decisions have been made.

Aisha desperately wanted to go to the local college after leaving school but her parents were very afraid for her safety. The family had strict ideas on how girls should be brought up and they felt she would be safer at home.

A meeting was arranged at the college when everyone was able to express their point of view. A Muslim member of staff was able to reassure the parents by talking through how the college was meeting the cultural needs of Muslim students. Aisha was able to start part time with a learning coach to help her.

Case history – 'Family Matters', National Development Team

Support systems and transition

A most important stage in the transition process is the time between a student leaving school and settling into their first job, course or training scheme. A lack of collaboration between professionals and agencies at this point means that school-leavers are even more vulnerable. There must be a good support system within which professionals working in partnership can co-ordinate support. Research on the experience of school-leavers with moderate learning difficulties and/or behaviour difficulties conducted at Lancaster University[2] suggested the following directions:

- improve training given to youth training staff to equip them with better skills for dealing with specific issues related to special school-leavers;
- extend the policy of statementing to enable special educational support to be offered more easily within training and further education;
- encourage communication between agencies such as the careers service, the probation service, social services and housing, to provide a more integrated support network.

A checklist for managers

◆ The person with a learning disability should be helped to contribute as much as possible at every stage in all decisions about his or her life

◆ An advocate should be appointed to contribute on behalf of the young person if they are unable to express their own view

◆ Parents, relatives and carers should be invited to attend transition planning meetings to contribute their unique knowledge of the person, and to share ideas

◆ Plan meetings at times and in places that are convenient to families and meet their particular needs

◆ Ensure that information is accurate and shared in advance to enable everyone to start from a similar information base

◆ Avoid duplication of information – it simply adds confusion

◆ Make sure everyone understands the purpose and rules of any meeting

◆ Record decisions and time scales for action

Real work, further education and other community-based opportunities must become part of each person's expectations for themselves as they leave school. If those opportunities are well planned and supported, then the stress of this most important period of life will diminish and positive anticipation of future opportunities can flourish.

References

1. Orlowska D. Parental participation in issues concerning their sons and daughters with learning disabilities. *Disability and Society* 1995; 10(4).

2. Armstrong D, Davies P. The transition from school to adulthood: aspirations and careers advice for young adults with learning difficulties. *British Journal of Special Education* 1995; 22(2).

Further reading

Department of Health *et al. Making Connections: A guide for agencies helping young people with disabilities make the transition from school to adulthood.*

Mount B, Ducharme G, Beeman P. *Person-Centred Development: A journey in learning to listen to people with disabilities.* Manchester (CT): Communitas, 1991.

Partners in Policy-making – Report of the first course. NDT, 1996.

Puddicombe B. *Days: In search of real alternatives to the Adult Training Centre.* London: Values into Action, 1992.

Shah R. *The Silent Minority* National Children's Bureau 1992, 1995.

The role of a school in Changing Days

IN 1930 HENRY MORRIS OPENED his first Village College at Sawston in South Cambridgeshire. In Morris's vision educational establishments should not only be for young formative minds but be available to all members of the local community throughout their lifetimes. Sawston Village College has developed very much as Morris would have hoped, being the cultural, sporting and learning centre for the local community.

Given this background it was logical that the community colleges of South Cambridgeshire, Sawston and Bottisham in particular, should form a part of the Changing Days work in Cambridgeshire.

Sawston College had already developed links with Cambridge social services, centred around the Compass Centre – a small service for people with learning difficulties based in the village. Through this connection it became an important partner in a pilot scheme to extend the locally-based service to include other people with learning difficulties who currently attend day centres in Cambridge. This provided a valuable opportunity to explore further how education and social services could work together.

Early in 1996 an exploratory meeting established a forum of voluntary and statutory groups committed to creating more local opportunities for people with learning difficulties in learning, leisure and work. The forum included community education staff, social services managers, representatives from local group homes, the leader of a self-advocacy group, a regional arts co-ordinator and the founder of a local trust which promotes and supports community businesses.

With the college as a base, it was relatively easy to establish learning opportunities. Using FEFC funding, a teacher and a learning assistant were employed to offer a validated life skills course to ten adults. Another FEFC funded course teaches independent living skills in a staff house on the college campus. A grant from South Cambridgeshire District Council enabled the purchase of specialist bowling and games equipment. Taster courses in aromatherapy, art and music have proved popular.

The cost of the tutors is largely covered by the course fees paid by participants. Some students choose to enrol in mainstream community

cont.

education courses. Support is provided by a mixture of paid and volunteer staff. Members of the local community who offer to support and partner a student with learning disabilities have their course fees waived, or can pursue another course free of charge.

By the end of 1996 the members of the initial community forum decided they could create even more opportunities in education, work and leisure if they broke free from the restrictions of statutory structures and in January 1997 Opportunities Unlimited (OUL) was born. The group's basic mission remained unchanged but independence gave it new vigour.

Cambridgeshire Social Services encouraged the expansion of OUL with a grant of £6,000. In March 1997, OUL appointed an employment Manager to develop sheltered employment opportunities. Sawston Village College offered gardening and decorating contracts and other employment opportunities have come from local businesses. OUL has also set up a

local self-advocacy group which meets weekly at the college. This group is increasingly influencing the development of OUL and members have joined the board of trustees. OUL recently received a lottery grant of £60,000 and a further £24,000 from a local charity, the Huntingdon Trust and has appointed a full-time co-ordinator.

This initiative made significant progress in a comparatively short time, aided by the involvement of people with a shared vision and the freedom offered by independent status. By creating a separate charity controlled through a broadly representative board of trustees, the members of the various statutory agencies could plan, unencumbered by the tensions and complexities which often characterise large bureaucracies.

The project has also shown how a school is able to make a contribution to reshaping community-based provision. South Cambridgeshire schools enjoy a very effective FEFC franchising system with local further education colleges which

enables them to support worthwhile and validated adult education classes. It is the school, sensitive to local needs, which designs the adult education programme and is able therefore to respond to initiatives such as the Sawston pilot scheme.

Also in the past decade schools have been given delegated budgets with the freedom to negotiate a wide range of service contracts including grounds maintenance, catering, caretaking, cleaning and elements of administration. This gives an enormous service base within which to create sheltered employment opportunities for people with learning difficulties.

All schools have the potential to contribute to the work of providing education, leisure and employment opportunities for women and men with learning difficulties. They have a bedrock of commitment to community evolution together with a wealth of experience in gaining grants from a range of funding agencies. ■

Chapter 11

Supported employment

Vision and Principles

Despite changes in our society in recent years, and high rates of unemployment in many parts of the country, work is still one of the major defining roles in our lives. It provides structure to our week, represents a forum for the pursuit of our interests, personal goals, and for the development of our social networks, as well as delivering the income by which we live. Although not the only way to pursue inclusion, people with learning difficulties who get jobs increase their potential for joining the mainstream of society.

Becoming an employee can affect positively the way people with learning difficulties view themselves, building their confidence and self-esteem. Becoming a paid worker and contributing member of society can also change the way their family and peer group see them.

Developing employment opportunities for people with learning difficulties involves:

- working towards inclusion in ordinary work settings;
- helping people find jobs which offer the same pay and terms and conditions as fellow employees doing comparable work;
- offering people the necessary support to function in the workplace;
- assisting those with severe and complex disabilities to find work and providing on-going support where required. (*Changing Days*, 1996)

Employment opportunities must become a part of the mainstream support offered to men and women with learning difficulties, not left to small agencies, inadequately funded, on 'the edge' of services. ■

Background

The architects of supported employment followed the principle that no one need be rejected for work, the onus being on the service to 'improve their game' to the point where they could find the right job and give proper support to make it work for both employer and worker. They felt progress would be greater if problems were the responsibility of the employment specialist, rather than a burden on the person with a disability.

Supported employment began with a series of demonstrations showing men and women with severe learning disabilities how careful application of behavioural training techniques could enable them to perform complex tasks and open the door to paid employment. In the years that followed, development progressed from effective task training, through commercial sales-driven job-finding approaches to the forging of partnerships with employers, assisting them to support workers with disabilities themselves, and was capped by the very best in sensitive person-centred planning. At its peak supported employment is a sophisticated and well tested technology. The stages in the supported employment process are summarised in Figure 1.

Strengths from a Changing Days viewpoint

Person-centred

The core of this supported employment process is person-centred. Its starting point is that each person is an individual. It celebrates their differences, discovers their interests and uses these to create an imaginative and workable job match. The process pays equal attention to analysing the job, the workplace, and the work culture. By collecting detailed information on both worker and workplace the supported employment process is able to make sophisticated job matches that suit the person's interests and take account of their abilities and disabilities. There are many times when even unrealistic ideas have been used as a base for job development which, shaped by discussion and short-term job experience to something more realistic, have retained the person's original intention.

Real jobs

Jobs found through supported employment are real jobs that employers need doing: jobs that someone else would be paid to do if the person with learning difficulties was not doing them themselves. Workers do not perform to a make-believe standard, they work to the same standard as everyone else. In good supported employment workers are contributing to the success of their employer's business and are viewed as an asset not a burden.

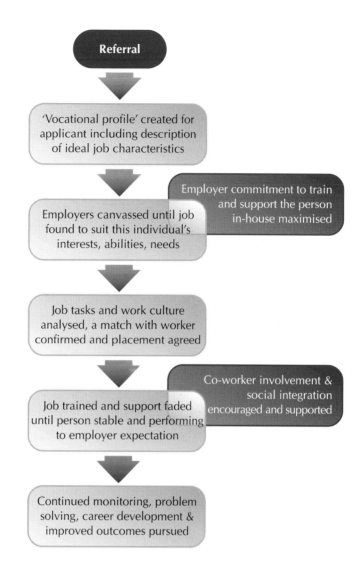

Fig. 1 Key stages in the supported employment process

Ordinary working life

Supported employment is about helping the person live an ordinary working life. It is about what people can do with help and appropriate training, not what is beyond them due to lack of experience and lack of knowledge. Training that begins only when the person is in their job is therefore more powerful than unsuitable pre-vocational training. Techniques such as task analysis and systematic instruction can close the gap between current ability and employer's requirement. On-the-job training also helps overcome the difficulty often faced by disabled people of transferring a task learned in one place to another and skills learned in one task to a similar task. An experienced trainer on site can, if necessary, adapt the way jobs are done and then use fading techniques to prevent the supported employee becoming reliant on them for cues and information.

Cheshire County Council Supported Employment Service

THE SERVICE WAS FORMED IN 1995 by amalgamating several small supported employment units and is now used by over 400 people throughout Cheshire.

Supported employment in Cheshire is a generic service, funded through service level agreements with the purchasers in each of the social services districts. The service has ten case holders (work placement officers) supported by 15 job coaches and is based in six local offices. Although the service is based on a supported employment model, emphasis is given to developing multi-agency approaches to delivery.

In addition to being a service provider, SES is actively involved in service development and system change, including community business developments, accredited staff training, and transition for young people both in the areas of disability and disadvantage. ∎

Contact: John Bottomley, Central Offices, Chester Road, Hartford, Cheshire CW8 2AB. Tel: 01606 301027.

Taking risks

Good supported employment will use information about a prospective worker gained from vocational profiling to plan around any risks he or she might face. A careful job match, health and safety examinations in the workplace, and contingency planning for problems will minimise risks to workers and co-workers. Precision teaching to high standards of consistency can bring potentially hazardous jobs well within the capability of some men and women with learning difficulties.

Promoting social contacts

Ordinary workplaces provide natural opportunities for people with disabilities to spend time with non-disabled colleagues. However, research shows that the traditional approach to supported employment which emphasises the role of the job coach can interfere with the development of this contact. Research also shows that employers are able and often willing to take on more of the training and support roles. Many agencies now provide advice and support directly to employers and co-workers, thus increasing the chance that supported employees get to know their colleagues and feel part of the workforce.

Increasing income

Finally, as in all paid jobs, supported employment has the potential to increase income and help people move out of the relative poverty of state welfare benefits.

The Humberston Trust

HUMBERSTON AIMS TO encourage the development of projects which facilitate employment opportunities for people often excluded from the labour market. It identifies and supports community businesses which offer disadvantaged people work experience, sheltered and open employment opportunities.

Humberston offers information about community enterprise, as well as advice about developing business ideas, marketing, legislation, writing business plans, raising finance, the benefits system, equal opportunities and training workshops. ■

Contact: Peter Durrant, Co-ordinator, 5 Kentings, Comberton, Cambridge CB3 7DT.
Tel: 01223 262 759; e-mail: thedurrants@cityscape.co.uk

Strengths for changing organisations

Supported employment has a number of strengths from the perspective of those managing day services change.

Cost-effectiveness

It does not require a fixed level of support, although input can be intensive and at first costly. However, with effective placement and training, many workers need less support over time which becomes less intensive for services and less costly. Decreasing involvement then enables staff to take on larger caseloads. The staff client ratios are comparable to a traditional day service model, even where these are based on provision in groups. Average costs per worker placed decrease over time to levels that compare with traditional day services.

Staffing

Managed properly, supported employment can reduce numbers served day in, day out by the day service, and give staff time for people who do not wish to pursue employment.

Attracts funding

As supported employment lies on the boundary between social services and employment, it is well placed to attract non-social care funding. European Social Fund resources, Employment Service funding through the Access to Work scheme, Rehabilitation Contracts as well as Training and Enterprise Council funding have all been obtained by some agencies. This money has helped services develop their funding base and employ more staff.

Project Career

PROJECT CAREER IS A TWO-YEAR programme funded through the European Social Fund to enable people with learning difficulties to explore the career of their choice through sampling a range of work placements. A career adviser draws up a personal development programme and provides direct support to people placed with employers, including training and liaison duties with trainees, employers, families and professional staff.

Local partnership

The overall management responsibility of the project lies with a sub-group of ACET (Agencies in Consortium for Education and Training) with representatives of:

- The Orchardville Society
- South and East Belfast Trust
- Training and Employment Agency
- Tor Bank and Glenveagh Schools
- Belfast Institute for Further and Higher Education.

A parents' council engages the support and expertise of parents and carers. The day-to-day managing of the project is the responsibility of the Orchardville Society.

Transnational partnership

Working with partners in other European member states, Project Career was set up to develop a transnational system which can be used in other member states and across other disability groups. Transnational partners are in Sweden, The Netherlands, Finland, the Republic of Ireland and Belgium. ■

For further information on Project Career contact: The Orchardville Society, 98 Fane Street, Belfast BT9 7BW. Tel: 01232 663289; fax: 01232 666079.

Strengthens social networks

Skills in vocational profiling, task training and developing natural support in the workplace can also help to link people into leisure and recreation networks within their communities.

Partnerships with employers

Connections made with local businesses through supported employment have other spin-offs for the day service changes. Some services have obtained 'investment in kind', such as consultancy on business planning to aid in the creation of small businesses.

Barriers to supported employment

Supported employment has many potential advantages for those organisations committed to Changing Days: readers will note the use of the word 'potential' here. While very significant to individuals, its contribution to promoting wider change has not always been as great as it might be, mainly because of barriers put up by national welfare and employment policies.

Welfare policies

The first major obstacle is the simplistic assumption in the welfare benefit system that people who are disabled cannot work, and people who can work are not disabled. Despite the Government's 'Welfare to Work' programme, there are no adequate bridges that enable people to move with confidence between welfare benefit income based on disability and an earned income. There are no tapering mechanisms that allow retention of benefit while increasing net income through earnings and no sliding scale to decrease benefit as earnings reach a living wage. Nor does the system recognise the fluctuating nature of certain disabilities, such as mental health problems, which means people are able to work for some periods and not others.

Many people have fought hard to gain the benefits they receive and under the current system getting a job can see them re-defined as no longer disabled. If they fall ill, lose their job, or their employer goes out of business, they can face long periods with little income as they fight to regain those previous benefits. Where eligibility tests have been tightened, as in the case of incapacity benefit, they may lose protected status and fail to regain their higher level benefits.

Who would risk this? While many do so, a large number of people and their families will not, and this creates knock-on effects for supported employment and those involved in day service change. Many will enter paid work only if their disabled status, and their welfare benefits, can be retained, even where the income from a paid job would outstrip benefit income. This is currently permissible if the person is classed as benefiting from 'therapeutic' work, and is eligible for an earnings disregard in respect of their benefits. The net amount they earn will be relatively small, and if they, and their employer, are to avoid exploitation, the hours they work will also be few. While even a small increase in income may be extremely useful to the individual, for those involved in day service change part-time work causes problems. A part-time job consumes the same amount of time and resources in vocational profiling and job finding as a full-time job. It does not replace a five-day-a-week day centre place and does not free staff to work with more people and develop new activities.

In addition, part-time jobs of less than 16 hours per week, and where the worker has no realistic prospect of moving off welfare benefit, will not attract funding from the Employment Service that might offset the cost of support.

> ### *Pause for thought*
>
> *We all know about the 'take your sons/daughters to work' days. Why not organise such a day with people with learning difficulties? Involve parents and others in taking one or two people along to their place of work. Don't leave 'work experience' just to the employment workers.*

Employment policies

The second barrier to change through supported employment is the nature of employment funding for prospective workers with disabilities. The introduction of the Access to Work scheme a few years ago opened up a potential source of money to help fund job coach support on the job. However, this scheme only covers the cost of on-the-job support, which is only part of the help people need. Vocational profiling, job finding, and job analysis – all essential to a good job match – are not covered by this funding. Even if all day services clients wanted to move into employment, were willing to relinquish their welfare benefits, and were eligible for Employment Service funding, core funding would still be needed from another source to achieve their employment.

TECs administer huge resources on behalf of the government to help tackle unemployment and promote full use of the skills of the workforce. Although there are imaginative schemes in place, the favoured mechanism here, as in Europe, is training for work. Such training generally does not suit many people with learning disabilities, and even those who do learn skills from these schemes and gain vocational qualifications often require additional help to find and keep a job. Supported employment is not seen as a legitimate intervention to fund by many TECs and few are funded purely to implement the supported employment process. Skilled agencies do obtain funding, but usually by representing what they do as training, or adding additional elements mainly to become eligible for funding.

Purchaser policies

A third set of obstacles arise from the way some social services departments handle funding of supported employment in day service change. This stems from pressures caused by reorganisation of local government and the implementation of wider community care policies, particularly the purchaser–provider split. The creation of unitary authorities has reduced the ability of purchasers to fund large-scale service developments. This means

National Initiative for Supported Employment (NISE)

STATUS EMPLOYMENT, A supported employment agency working with people with learning difficulties, has developed this initiative as a partnership between its own organisation, government agencies and large business.

The aim is to significantly increase the implementation of supported employment and the numbers of people getting jobs by assigning consultants to work exclusively on behalf of one organisation.

The consultants carry out the usual tasks associated with supported employment – vocational profiling, identifying potential jobs, induction training, on-going support – but also offer information and support to all staff in the organisation.

The first NISE partnership was funded by Sainsbury's and South London TEC. Two Status consultants worked with the 14 Sainsbury stores in the area, identifying jobs and training and supporting employees. Discussion is now under way to expand the service across 66 stores in the south of England with potentially 200 vacancies for employees with learning difficulties. ■

Contact: Status Employment Ltd, Airport House, Purley Way, Croydon, Surrey CR0 0XZ.
Tel: 0181 681 3178; fax: 0181 686 2469

supported employment agencies have had to negotiate contracts with several authorities to retain their funding where once they had just one contract.

In some cases agency staff have been allocated directly to clients from particular authorities. This misunderstands the reality of effective supported employment. Allocating staff direct to clients ignores the difficulty of providing cover for job coaches during sickness and holidays. It ignores the fact that each person is unpredictable and that vocational profiling, job finding, placement and training take varying lengths of time. Staff become available for new referrals at different times, and not in the order funders might like.

Specific allocation of staff ignores the specialties that develop within teams that may be required for any particular worker, irrespective of where they live. Finally, it ignores personality and restricts the ability to match the right person to each client. Supported employment needs the flexibility to allocate work across teams.

Allocations of new contracts and agreements are sometimes the reason why agencies serve only people with learning disabilities who are already social service clients. This can mean that people who have become dissatisfied with social services and left the system are sometimes denied access to supported employment. It also limits the ability of agencies to attract income from other funders such as Department of Employment PACT teams. Some social services departments see this as a misuse of their core funding rather than a step to obtaining solid funding for supported employment as well as a source of additional staff to add flexibility to the team.

These agreements can also specify unrealistic numbers of people to be served in the early years of a supported employment agency. Establishing links with employers and the experience needed to deliver a high number of good-quality jobs takes time. Varying degrees of disability will also affect the amount of time needed to place people successfully. Little thought is given to the restrictive effect of the benefit system mentioned earlier on the achievable balance of full-time and part-time jobs. All of this can result in unjustified disappointment by funders with the performance of supported employment and failure to manage effectively its contribution to the change in day services.

Differing cultures

Ironically, a fourth set of barriers to the success of supported employment comes from the gap between social service culture and the business world. The principle concern within social care organisations is the client and their family. But supported employment has two clients: the employer and the supported worker. Supported employment developed as part of day service change risks valuing client outcomes above all others and not respecting the needs of the employer. Companies are not philanthropic organisations: they have different aims, face different pressures, and respond to different arguments. Placement of people with learning difficulties must make sound business sense in terms of good worker performance and a cohesive workforce. The concept must be sold to them in a language and style that they recognise and value. Employers need to see supported employment agencies as relevant to their endeavours and professionals from social care traditions are often at a disadvantage here.

Overcoming the barriers

Changes in funding structure

Helping supported employment secure a wider funding base and move from pilot schemes to the mainstream service must be the next aim. For supported employment to flourish, however, a partnership must develop between legislators and those providing employment support. Mainstream employment funding must be restructured to ensure that all of the supported employment process can be funded centrally. Without this all people with disabilities will be deprived of appropriate help, and disadvantaged in relation to other long-term unemployed job seekers.

Revisions of benefits systems

Welfare benefit systems also need revision to enable people with disabilities to move with some confidence into paid employment without suffering disproportionate risk of financial ruin. If this reform is achieved, many will gain, including the tax payer, as men and women with disabilities become tax payers rather than welfare benefit claimants.

Further reading

Bass M *et al. Supported Employment for People with Learning Difficulties.* Findings, Social Care Research 86. York: Joseph Rowntree Foundation, 1996.

Beyer S, Kilsby M. Supported employment in Britain. *Learning Disability Review* 1997; 2(2).

Open for Business: A best practice guide in access. Employers' Forum on Disability in partnership with the Bucknall Group, 1997.

Steele D. Is the honeymoon over? *Community Living* 1996; October:17–18.

Chapter 12

Access to continuing education

Vision and Principles

'The role of education is crucial in providing vocational and work-related training opportunities for people with learning difficulties.

Educational opportunities should be an integral part of the individual planning process and should have a clear purpose, whether related to employment, leisure or personal development.

Colleges and adult education should be seen as part of community provision, offering structured and individually tailored educational and training opportunities with appropriate support. The emphasis should be on progression: that is, devising a planned route through from one stage to another, with in-built preparation and transition arrangements.' (Changing Days, 1996).

The book *Changing Days* gave a background picture to the education scene in the UK and outlined some of the opportunities available to people with learning difficulties. A major challenge then, as now, was how to make educational provision more inclusive for people with disabilities. Although a substantial number of people use ordinary adult and further education facilities, too often they remain segregated from other students.

The Government is making education a top priority and has set up an advisory group on adult learning. It seems an opportune time therefore to redouble our efforts to increase real educational opportunities for people with learning difficulties. ■

A few snapshots

Elizabeth goes to an adult education evening class to learn flower arranging. A volunteer goes with her to offer any extra support required. Both of them learn together alongside non disabled people. Elizabeth is lucky to live in one of the few areas where the local authority and social services fund this type of scheme. She says, 'It's a good experience – to get out of the house, learn new things and meet new people.'

Stan is good at woodwork. He is part of an NVQ course at a city college. None of the other students has learning difficulties. Stan has made a beautiful casement clock, which was displayed in the end-of-year exhibition. He does not use expressive speech but communicates through smiles and grunts. The college provides a support worker, who describes herself as 'part of the class ... I don't just want to be known as Stan's support worker.' At break times Stan stays with the other students and is accepted in the group in his own right. His parents say that he really enjoys college: 'He likes to come to college. Yesterday, when we told him that the college was shut [for the end of term], he wasn't pleased about it.' It is hoped to find a work placement for Stan as a next step via the local supported employment scheme.

Renu goes to an Asian studies course for people with learning difficulties at college. The course looks at different Asian countries and cultures. Shopping for Asian food and looking at different festivals are among the topics they have covered. Renu says, 'It's important to learn about India because me and my sister haven't been before ... I've seen video, films but that's it.'

These snapshots give an idea of how education can be a route to joining in with learning in the community alongside non disabled people or how learning can offer the chance for personal development, as in the example celebrating different Asian cultures. The opportunities for inclusion described in the first two examples are still unfortunately the exception rather than the norm. The majority of provision for adults with learning difficulties is still segregated or 'discrete'. Classes aimed at Black and Asian students with learning difficulties are rare and it is no surprise to find that such students are still under-represented in the college population as a whole.[1]

Wigan and Leigh College

WIGAN AND LEIGH COLLEGE has been developing arrangements which centre on the individual student's progression through vocational courses to training and employment. Thirty support workers, paid by the hour, enable people to take part in mainstream classes.

Link courses are established with local special schools, which aids the transition for school-leavers. Students can then choose a full-time vocational course.

After completing the course, individuals can select to use the college's supported employment service rather than the local day service. This offers training, work experience, and unpaid and paid employment, matching individual needs and preferences. Job trainers and support workers offer on-the-job support as required.

A joint college/social services project has also been developed, providing additional training for individuals before they are referred to the employment service, should this be necessary. ■

Contact: Kathryn Green, Wigan and Leigh College, Wigan Campus, PO Box 53, Parsons Walk, Wigan WW1 1 RS. Tel: 01942 501 501.

The Further and Higher Education Act (1992)

The FHE Act (1992) brought major changes when it was implemented in April 1993. Colleges became independent from local authority control and had their curriculum defined by the legislation. The Further Education Funding Council (FEFC) was set up to administer the new system in England, with a separate FEFC for Wales. Courses which the FEFC will fund are listed in the section on funding. A new requirement was an emphasis on progression and accreditation where possible, with courses restricted to vocational or academic subjects. Learning for fun or personal development suddenly became more difficult. The split between vocational and non vocational learning is an artificial divide; for example cake decorating could be seen as frivolous, but some people go on to make a living from making cakes. Hopefully, the new Government group on adult learning will tackle some of these issues. Many LEAs have faced savage cuts in recent times. They are legally required to offer 'adequate' provision for all adult learners but quite what is meant by adequacy remains undefined. As adult education is not a statutory service, unlike schools, it is an easy target for cuts.

Still a Chance to Learn?[2] found that provision for young adults with moderate learning difficulties boomed under the new system following the FHE Act. However, those with more severe or profound learning difficulties were less fortunate. Older adults too were starting to lose out. The curriculum had narrowed to fit in with FEFC criteria, meaning that things like music, art and a women's group had gone. Planning and collaboration had suffered due to competition between colleges.

ACET (AGENCIES IN CONSORTIUM for Education and Training) formed in 1992, is a group of organisations committed to working together for the benefit of people with learning difficulties in South & East Belfast. It includes South & East Belfast Health and Social Services Trust, the Orchardville Society (parents' organisation), two special schools, two colleges of further education, the Training and Employment Agency, a local employers' representative and a number of voluntary agencies working with other groups of disabled people. Its key issues for the next three years are:

- Effective and accredited training for people with disabilities
- Transition from childhood to adulthood
- Community attitudes
- Travel
- Supported employment
- Training for carers and staff.

Why ACET?

Some ACET members had been working together for many years but by the early 90s realised that a more concerted effort was needed to really see significant change in people's lives. People with learning difficulties were rarely achieving recognised qualifications or moving on to employment, and because they were not being supported to move on, the whole system was becoming jammed.

The Work and Life Skills Programme

ACET's first achievement was a user-centred training programme, written to nationally accredited standards and capable of being run across agencies to meet the specific needs of individuals. This gave the consortium an excellent opportunity to explore in a very practical way how to pool their joint skills and resources and what organisational challenges might thus arise, such as transport, accountability and funding. Joint training days, shared tasks (jointly writing modules, joint field trips), inter-agency secondments, and joint project management have proved invaluable tools in developing mutual understanding. Because the programme is designed around the needs of individuals not institutions, the overall outcomes for people are much improved.

Keeping a local focus

To begin with, the consortium limited themselves to the South & East Belfast area and to agencies already working in education and training. It was felt that:

- inter-agency and consortium working were new concepts and needed to be tested carefully and properly understood;
- too many members to start with and too many different approaches might hinder progress;
- confining activity to the local area was more likely to stimu-

late a person-centred, community-based approach.

The challenge was to create a way of working together which kept people on track despite the continuous pressure from the wider needs of their own organisations. This was achieved through shared and stated vision. Members needed to understand why they were there, what they sought to achieve, what they were expected to contribute and what they hoped for in return. Fears of loss of territory or exploitation had to be addressed and sharing of resources, learning and knowledge encouraged. Considerable time and energy were spent on preparing the vision and values, which were then publicly launched in a jointly written document. Again and again this document has proved invaluable in times of uncertainty and in making decisions on conflicts of interest. These 'user-centred' values and vision which people physically put their names to are at the very heart of the process.

A supportive framework

The most productive elements to aid inter-agency working have been constructive ideas from staff based on real people's needs and commitment from senior managers. From the start it was essential that senior managers from all organisations were actively involved. This meant they had to allocate considerable time from their already busy schedules.

cont.

Financing new options

As in other areas of the UK much of the initial funding to develop alternatives was short-term and from a range of different sources, such as European funding, local community development money and lottery money. The challenge for all ACET members is how to acquire longer-term funding. This is not easy and probably never will be, but experience shows that when agencies work together, they develop the capacity to make better use of what is already available, to push back boundaries, and to exploit new potential.

Celebrating success

In 1990 no-one with a learning disability achieved a nationally accredited qualification and no-one got a job. In 1997 an awards night was held in a large Belfast hotel. During the year, 71 people with learning difficulties received accredited awards and four people moved on into employment. The potential of partnership was becoming visible in practice. ■

Contact: Hugh Connor, Head of Adult Services, South & East Belfast Health and Social Services Trust, Trust Headquarters, Knockbracken Healthcare Park, Saintfield Road, Belfast BT8 8BH. Tel: 01232 790673; fax: 01232 796632.

Inclusive learning and the Tomlinson Committee

The FEFC set up a three-year committee, chaired by Professor John Tomlinson, which produced a major report in September 1996, entitled *Inclusive Learning*.[3] This long and detailed report reviews existing provision and contains major recommendations for education for adults with learning difficulties and/or disabilities. The principal recommendations relate to:

- inclusive learning: this is not straightforward 'inclusion' but, as Tomlinson writes in the foreword, matching the learner to the situation: 'The first step is to determine the best possible learning environment, given the individual student and learning task ... for those with a learning difficulty the resulting educational environment will often be in an integrated setting'.
- under-representation of particular groups, to include those with profound/multiple learning difficulties
- redefining progression routes
- developing a pre-foundation award to offer an entry level certificate
- setting up a framework for collaboration to improve planning
- funding
- improving teaching and learning
- the quality initiative: improving teacher education/staff development

The FEFC consulted colleges, LEAs and others on the main recommendations, which were overwhelmingly supported. In July 1997 the FEFC announced initial funding for the quality initiative. In the academic year 1997–8, £1m was invested in a programme

A university challenge

ANGLIA POLYTECHNIC UNIVERSITY has launched a personal portfolio programme which provides an opportunity for people with learning difficulties to take part in higher education. A student with learning difficulties and a non-disabled student work together as a partnership. They identify some aspect of their lives that they wish to address and make a formal presentation of the issues. They are registered as part-time students and can use the full range of university facilities. All students can submit their work for academic validation. ∎

Contact: Tom Hewitt or Andy Stevens, Anglia Polytechnic University, Globe House, Rivermead Campus, Chelmsford, Essex. CM1 1SG. Tel: 01245 493 131, ext.4230

designed to generate a bank of materials for national staff development. The idea will be for all college staff and managers to become aware of the needs of adults with learning difficulties and/or disabilities as a more inclusive approach is adopted. The emphasis will be on individual learners and not on labels.

Funding possibilities

The following list provides some ideas of how continuing education for adults with learning difficulties is funded. Most places use a number of sources of funds to support their provision.

Further Education Funding Council

The FEFC funds designated courses listed in part of the FHE Act (1992) called 'Schedule 2'. Adults with learning difficulties get a specific mention and are eligible for funding under the heading of 'courses in independent living and communication skills for students with learning difficulties'.

Progression towards other Schedule 2 courses is required. Other courses listed under Schedule 2 include vocational courses (i.e. job related), academic courses such as GCSEs or 'A' levels, literacy, maths, English as a second language and Welsh. Access to higher education courses is also listed.

An FEFC report, *Learning Works: Widening participation in further education,*[4] recommended that colleges should cater for a much wider clientele. Coupled with the *Inclusive Learning* report, the recommendations make a powerful case on behalf of excluded or marginalised groups.

Local education authorities

Local education authorities fund adult education classes. Some of them include integrated learning opportunities for those with learning difficulties, such as the one which Elizabeth attends. Others have classes just for adults with learning difficulties. Some provision is well developed. Other areas have little. Owing to cuts in funding, class availability varies enormously, depending on where you live. LEAs can and do run FEFC-funded provision in the Schedule 2 categories listed above.

Other sources of funding

Colleges and LEAs often seek funding from a variety of sources. The following have all been successfully approached:

- European Community resources such as the European Social Fund or Leonardo programme
- health authority/trust
- social services
- training and enterprise councils
- voluntary organisations
- joint funding.

Research published in *Still A Chance to Learn?*[2] found that a higher proportion of colleges than LEAs received money from TECs or from Europe. It was more common for LEAs than colleges to obtain funding from health, social services and voluntary organisations.

Work in progress

A great deal is happening at present concerning education and adults with learning difficulties. Following the Disability Discrimination Act, there is a new legal requirement for colleges and LEAs in England and Wales to produce disability statements outlining their provision. This will be an important step forward for students with learning difficulties and/or disabilities.

NIACE, the national organisation for adult learning, has two projects under way, results from which are to be published in autumn 1998. *All Things Being Equal?* will report on provision in continuing education for marginalised groups of adults with learning difficulties, such as older adults, people with profound/multiple learning difficulties and those from Black and other minority ethnic groups. The second NIACE project, in

Newham Sixth Form College

NEWHAM SIXTH FORM COLLEGE supports the borough of Newham's policy for inclusive education which aims to give all students access to mainstream education wherever appropriate. The college's mission states that they will:

- actively promote equality of opportunity for all students
- provide quality student-centred learning to encourage all students to achieve their best

• offer a support service which will identify and respond to individual learning needs

Specialist staff on their inclusive learning team enable students to get the advice, support and teaching they require which best suits their needs. Support offered includes:

- access to a wide range of academic and vocational programmes with all other college students
- support workshops and support groups

- learning support assistants – including communicators/ signers
- aids and equipment
- special examination arrangements

Most students with additional needs have a support tutor as well as their mainstream tutor to help them identify their requirements, set targets and monitor progress. ■

Contact: Steve West, Newham Sixth Form College, Prince Regent Lane, London E13 8SG. Tel 0171 473 4110. Fax: 0171 511 9463.

collaboration with CHANGE, will produce materials aimed at supporting people with learning difficulties who want to do training. The pack, backed by the Department of Health, will also have a video and audiotape version funded by the National Lottery Charities Board. The course will be accredited by the National Open College Network and, as a vocational course, should be eligible for FEFC funding if the DofEE put it on the approved list.

The *Inclusive Learning* report now has an implementation committee at the Further Education Funding Council, to advise the FEFC on how to put the report's practical recommendations into practice. The staff development 'quality initiative' will make a good start with £1m allocated over 1997/98.

Checklist for staff and others wanting to help adults with learning difficulties to access education

◆ Build allies and partnerships when you are trying to get things going

◆ Don't be put off because of lack of funding. Use existing money differently

◆ Support users to get involved, for example, in college committees, training of staff

◆ Make sure that students have support to make informed choices about their learning. Ask if taster sessions can be provided

◆ Find the right class for each person, not people to fill a class. Don't turn up on enrolment evening with ten people and say, 'It's their *right* to join the pottery class!' The appropriate support needs planning and you can turn an opportunity for integration into another segregated ghetto by block booking

◆ Let the student choose something that interests them and they want to learn. People have been sent to literacy classes 'because it is on their needs chart' and then failed to make progress due to lack of motivation.

◆ Ask for accessible information. Many colleges and LEAs still do not offer prospectuses with large print, clear language and pictures or photos. If there isn't one, offer to do it together and involve users.

◆ Ask for self advocacy courses to be arranged if there is a local need. An increase in self advocacy courses is recommended by both the *Inclusive Learning* and the *Building Expectations*[5] reports. Use this as ammunition.

◆ Ensure that support workers understand the importance of their role and have training and guidelines on how to offer effective support to students in a class. (In one class recently, the support worker sat at the back filing her nails!)

◆ Think carefully about transport arrangements. They can be a major obstacle.

◆ Offer to help education staff with relevant training inputs to their staff development programme. This can be a fair exchange. Set up joint training if you can. For example, the NIACE staff development packs can be studied and delivered in a multi-agency context.

◆ Consider progression planning. A lot of people with learning difficulties get recycled around the system doing endless courses called 'Next Steps' or 'New Horizons' without getting anywhere very fast.

◆ Understand that tutors of mainstream classes may have little experience of people with learning difficulties. They need support to overcome misapprehensions and include students successfully.

References

1. *Mapping Provision: The provision of and participation in further education by students with learning difficulties and/or disabilities.* London: HMSO, 1997.

2. Sutcliffe J, Macadam M. *Still A Chance to Learn? A report on the impact of the Further and Higher Education Act (1992) on education for adults with learning difficulties.* NIACE, 1996.

3. *Inclusive Learning. The report of the Further Education Funding Council Learning Difficulties and/or Disabilities Committee.* HMSO, 1996.

4. Kennedy H. *Learning Works: Widening participation in further education.* FEFC, 1997

5. *Building Expectations: Opportunities and services for people with a learning disability.* Mental Health Foundation, 1996.

Further reading and resources

Hood P. *Aspects of the 1992 Further Education Act and Students with Learning Difficulties and Disabilities. A guide for staff working in the health and social services and independent sector.* Manchester: National Development Team, 1997.

Learning Disability: Working as equal people. The Open University. Walton Hall, Milton Keynes MK7 6AA. Tel: 01908 653743.

NIACE staff development packs, which are linked to National Open College Network accreditation:

Sutcliffe J. *Enabling Learning: A student-centred approach to teaching students with learning difficulties* (Staff development pack). NIACE, 1996.

Sutcliffe J. *Towards Inclusion: Developing integrated education for adults with learning difficulties* (Staff development pack). NIACE, 1996.

NIACE publications on education for adults with learning difficulties:

Learners as Trainers (working title). Pack funded by the Department of Health and the National Lottery Charities Board to support adults with learning difficulties to be trainers. NIACE/CHANGE. Publication date: autumn 1998

Sutcliffe J, Jacobsen Y. *All Things Being Equal? Equal opportunities and adults with learning difficulties in continuing education.* Publication date: autumn 1998

Chapter 13

Making it happen for people with complex disabilities

Vision and Principles

> 'Inclusion in the life of ordinary communities must be the goal for everyone with a disability, including those who may need intensive support in order to do so because of the complexity of their disabilities, or because they behave in ways which may be risky and threatening to themselves and/or other people. Service providers generally struggle to understand and meet their needs. However, we are learning more and more about how we can do this better.'
>
> (Changing Days, 1996)

The principles are the same as for people who are more independent:

- Start with the hopes and dreams of the person
- Focus on abilities rather than disabilities
- Give top priority to developing effective communication
- Support each person to be actively involved in their choice of lifestyle
- Meet the special needs of each person in the least special way.

Many men and women with complex needs spend much of the week doubly segregated in special care units based in day centres. Moving from this to supporting each person to participate in the community is often difficult and time-consuming. The good news is that more and more success stories are proving it can be done.

Progressive services are emerging where men and women with complex needs are being supported individually in the community without a building base, getting jobs, going to college and participating in a range of activities in purposeful ways. This follows good person-centred planning, excellent staff training and growing awareness from the community of the need to welcome people with complex disabilities into the mainstream of life. (See also Chapter 5.)

There is an increasing number of people with high support needs nationally, including those who have non-verbal communication, who will be entering the service in the near future. Unless we begin to develop staff skills now as well as the capacity of organisations to support this group, we won't achieve the quality of life that they are seeking. ■

The current scene

Across the UK the quality of day opportunities for men and women with complex physical and intellectual disabilities is disappointing. Most of them are still being supported either in special care units or within an NHS Trust residential facility.

- Many people with complex needs have great difficulty in communicating those needs and this limits their opportunities to challenge service systems.
- Service providers still rely on building-based services. There is scepticism about coping without a building, especially for those who have major health care needs.
- Most people spend their time in groups, which limits the individual attention they receive.
- Staff are often unskilled and unclear about what they can or should do and end up focusing on personal care. As a result they spend less time communicating with people who have complex needs than with those who are more able.
- The approach to care tends to concern itself with physical well-being and less account is taken of emotional, social and educational needs.
- Privacy and dignity are not always considered.
- Social isolation is common with very little opportunity for in-depth relationships.

People with complex needs are particularly vulnerable in regard to their general health. Many have difficulty expressing and describing symptoms. A study by the Roeher Institute in Canada showed that 30 per cent had an undiagnosed hearing loss. Much work needs to be done to enable primary health care teams to meet the needs of this group.[1] (See Chapter 14 for detailed discussion of health care needs.)

Key issues

Communication

Effortless, quick and accurate communication is one of the most complex and important skills of human beings. To be denied that skill severely limits our opportunities to make relationships, develop our personalities, and express our thoughts and fears. Many people with severe learning difficulties don't use language either by speech or sign and rely on interpretation by others of their unique methods of communication in order to be understood. Those who work with adults with severe learning difficulties have always seen it as their role to promote effective communication skills, but many organisations don't give enough priority to providing the necessary training opportunities. The day-to-day relationship between the person who uses services and his or her support worker is of the utmost importance, yet it often seems that front-line staff are left without any real guidance.[2]

Improving communication

HACKNEY SOCIAL SERVICES AND City & Hackney Community Services NHS Trust undertook a study with adults with severe learning difficulties and limited communication.[4] The main aim was to find ways in which communication could be improved. The study showed that:

- a high proportion of people had hearing and visual difficulties which had previously been undetected
- of the 66 service users seen, 15 needed alternative or augmented communication
- 16 of the 66 would be helped by Makaton symbols
- having good support for hearing aid management and regular links with NHS service providers for hearing impairments is essential
- staff must have access to augmentative and alternative communication techniques and have their training regularly updated
- people must have regular reviews of their visual and hearing difficulties
- finding out how the person currently communicates is best done by starting with people who know the service user
- there are a number of warning signs that indicate that the person has a hearing deficit or visual loss
- the most common form of communication that was found to be helpful was objects of reference: 23 of the 66 people seen were in this category
- the use of a light-writer, visual calendars and symbols can all be helpful
- best use should be made of Health Call, a domiciliary optical service which is free to people receiving benefits. They will identify a number of visual difficulties including long and short sightedness, cataracts, glaucoma and squints, diabetes and infections. ∎

Contact Tel: 01908 691919 (0181 370 5222)

In a report, *Face to Face*,[3] these issues are explored and a number of ideas suggested about how working relationships can be constructed to offer better opportunities for users to be understood. Often small technological advances or new techniques are put forward as solutions to the shortcomings in services.

Facilitated communication

Facilitated communication has been shown to be an effective tool for helping people with communication difficulties. Despite much scepticism it continues to attract a great deal of interest. The definition used by many practitioners in the UK is 'a strategy that may enable some people with severe communication impairment to point to objects, pictures, symbols, words or letters for communication purposes'.[5] A facilitator provides physical support to help stabilise or control movement. The facilitator aims to teach independent pointing skills and fade support as soon as possible.

Carly's story: the use of multi-media profiling

Carly goes to the Orchardville Centre in Belfast. She spends a lot of time lying on a beanbag and needs to be fed through a gastric tube. The challenge was how to give Carly a voice and help her communicate. Through Changing Days, staff heard about multi-media profiling and visited Acting Up* in Hackney. They started to video Carly, recording her ways of communicating, her eye movements, noises and chuckles, her facial expressions and body movements. These are described and also interpreted. A profile has been built up using pictures from her past and talking to people who know her. Carly enjoys the experience and has begun to respond to the sound of her own voice on the video. She can activate the computer programme by the tone of her voice.

This information is invaluable to new staff in getting to know Carly's unique ways of communicating. Over time staff are building up a much better picture of who she is, how she is and what she needs and wants.

For information about Acting Up, see Chapter 7

Challenging behaviour

People with severe reputations for challenging behaviour are frequently described as 'not ready' for the community. But the problem often rests with how services approach and support the individual. We look at needs and develop services in terms of the person's deficits and disabilities, whereas it is essential to start from the opposite end of the spectrum – from their strengths and abilities. We need a system which starts with the individual, ensures that we understand them and then helps others meet that person rather than their reputation.

Many people with challenging behaviour have modest but fundamental basic needs which are not being met. We are seeking to understand the circumstances that are necessary for that person's happiness and fulfilment. This may take time to learn but can be achieved.

Community Resource Service: London Borough of Hackney

THE SERVICE WAS SET UP IN 1994 to support people with complex needs. A team of six workers and their manager provide individual support to about twenty people to participate in community activities of their choosing.

There is no building base. People no longer attend a day centre. They are supported one-to-one for sessions e.g. half a day at a time. Over a period, people have developed the skills to use public transport, leisure facilities, adult education and ordinary places in the community such as cafes, restaurants and theatres. For some people the need for support will diminish, for others it will continue. *See also Chapter 5 – Getting a life, not a building.* ■

Supporting people with challenging behaviour requires changing the way we think and work. It challenges our old approaches. It involves helping staff think differently about a person's future. To start with, providers may need to invest in a lot of extra time to enable staff to understand each individual, experiment with different ideas and develop a flexible array of supports. Over the long term this means less time, reduced costs and a much better quality of life for the person.

While people with severe reputations have the greatest need for a personal network, many have little family involvement and no friends. Developing a personal network may take a long time but is an essential part of achieving a better life for them. Sometimes there are people from an individual's past who are happy to be asked. They might be long-lost family members or staff from the institution where they used to live.

Implementing a person-centred plan may appear straightforward. However, as Michael Smull says,[2] it can take two years for a provider to move from thinking of 'services' to 'supports'. Changing the attitudes and practices of staff takes time. Changing corporate cultures takes even longer.

New opportunities may be available under the Direct Payments scheme or through setting up a trust for an individual which can be accountable for their funding when it is passed over from a statutory agency (see 'A circle of support as a trust').

Jane and the recycling scheme

Ryefields Centre, Ross-on-Wye, Herefordshire closed their special care unit and now support people to join in with the rest of the day centre and participate in a range of activities in the community. This change increased expectations around people who had been in the unit and revealed new abilities and talents. For one person, the change from special care was dramatic. Jane had attended the special care unit five days a week. For most of her time there, she moved around on her knees and this was accepted as the best mobility she could manage. When the special care unit closed Jane was encouraged to participate with staff and other service users in a recycling scheme in the village. She was given the job of pushing a shopping trolley while others loaded it with newspapers and drinks cans, and it was found she could walk considerable distances using the trolley as support.

Success in supporting people with severe reputations requires skill in planning and implementation alongside commitment and tenacity. The commitment is to the person not to the service. People need to work in a network so there are a number of allies supporting the individual in his or her journey into the community. People with severe reputations can be supported in life-styles of their own choosing. The tasks are complex but can be reduced to seeking the answers to five questions. We need to know:

- what is the individual's desired life-style?
- what supports are required to achieve that life-style with reasonable assurances that the safety of the individual and those around them are accounted for?
- who can provide this support, looking to community resources wherever possible?
- how can the necessary support be paid for?
- how will we know if our efforts are working?

Risk taking

Taking measured risk is essential to help people develop new skills and enjoy life to the full. Sensible but flexible risk-taking policies are important to help carers, staff and people who use services to agree potential areas of difficulty and how much risk will be taken.

It is often presumed that people with learning difficulties do not understand risk and have no sense of danger. But in many cases this may only be because the person has been so protected from taking risks that they have never had the chance to develop these skills.

The positive sound of breaking glass

Johrn was young man with a well-known reputation for breaking windows. One-to-one support over a period of time was focused on preventing him from inflicting damage to buildings and to himself. The regime became tighter and more controlling and John's behaviour was causing increasing concern. Then it was agreed to try turning the 'problem' on its head. Could John's obvious enjoyment of breaking glass be turned into a socially valued skill?

John had made it known that he would like to have a job, like his brothers and sisters. A job was found in a local glass recycling plant and now with the help of a job coach, John spends part of his week breaking glass. He enjoys the noise, the atmosphere and the fact he is doing something useful. His habit of breaking windows at home has greatly decreased. Clearly, John is happier, has greater self-esteem and sees himself as a more valued person.

Fully involving each person in looking at their own situation and understanding the risks is an important developmental process in itself.

Staff, users and carers need to agree a set of guiding principles which will enable staff to be flexible in their approach to risk-taking according to the needs of each individual. A difficult situation in the community may pose a risk for one person but not for another. It is essential to support professionals, carers and users through the agreed policies and procedures and to keep people who use services at the centre of the process.[6]

A circle of support as a trust

Brian and I first met nearly five years ago. Brian was living in an upstairs flat on a busy main road in London. I lived in rural Suffolk. Brian shared the flat with another person who had a learning difficulty, which didn't always work well.

The only activity staff said Brian liked was walking in the countryside. As he had no garden and the road was only a few feet from his door, it seemed like a good idea to invite him to my home where there are plenty of good walks nearby. What started as the odd weekend visit turned into a regular pattern whenever we both had a few spare days. Brian quickly showed he had many other interests and likes. Travelling in the car was always a favourite. Walking, drinking, cafes, music and pubs, but especially meeting other people were others.

In London things were not going well. Brian's flat was in a bad state. He was not getting the support he needed with his personal care and with managing his diabetes. Things came to a head when it was suggested that Brian have all his teeth out under general anaesthetic. But this brings added risk for any diabetic and I felt that with proper care Brian could save most of his teeth.

Brian had few friends and no contact with any family in London. He had made a number of good friends in Suffolk and developed an active social life. It seemed time to think about a move. Brian's friends were all committed to helping him live his life as he wanted. To enable a move and to ensure that he would retain control over his service, they formed a trust. As trustees they negotiated with the service purchaser for money so that Brian could employ his own support using the trust.

Brian does not use speech and needs a lot of daily support but he does know what he likes and doesn't like and has very clear opinions about who supports him. We found four people Brian was happy with. They do not work in short shifts. Brian likes people for a little longer than that so they usually spend two or three days together at a time. They enable him to lead the life he wants while providing the support he needs.

Having trustees from Brian's circle is a great protection. They ensure he gets the sort of service he wants. Brian and his wishes are therefore at the heart of decisions about his life and support, unhampered by other considerations. The system has many

cont.

safeguards that act very quickly when things go wrong. For instance, a couple of people who worked for Brian were found to be incompatible; this was quickly noticed and they were replaced.

The difference for Brian has been significant. He is now having treatment at a dentist using only local anaesthetic. He still travels a lot and has recently bought a new caravanette, his first trip being to Slovenia and Croatia to meet up again with old acquaintances.

Planning for life

Making community care a reality for people with complex needs demands particularly intensive and sensitive service planning, targeting and development. *Planning for life,*[7] a report from the Social Services Inspectorate, identifies the following action points to assist statutory and non-statutory agencies to develop quality services.

Checklist for managers

1. Integrated services: are services co-ordinated across agencies?
Do you:
◆ Clarify responsibilities within and between agencies?
◆ Produce joint principles, policies and budgets?
◆ Convene a multi-agency forum developing policies and services?
◆ Establish joint training programmes?
◆ Set up a cross-agency quality assurance programme?
◆ Share information across agencies for planning and commissioning?

2. User empowerment: are people who have profound intellectual difficulties and limited ability to communicate enabled to express their views and assume control over their lives?
Do you:
◆ Underpin services with shared value systems?
◆ Provide accurate, accessible information?
◆ Encourage the use of independent advocates?
◆ Develop quality standards based on user satisfaction criteria?
◆ Recognise that independence entails a measure of risk?
◆ Acknowledge the separate needs of relatives and friends?

cont.

3. Life planning: do you ensure the continuity of services towards agreed goals throughout the life of the individual?

Do you:

◆ Create a life book that follows the user throughout life?

◆ Set realistic and measurable short and longer term goals?

◆ Designate a named individual to co-ordinate services?

◆ Ensure that life planning takes place in a community care context?

◆ Consider long term resource implications of complex multiple disability?

◆ Ensure that meaningful day time activity is addressed in individual plans?

4. Specialist support: do you provide a range of flexibly delivered, specialist activities for a variety of disciplines?

Do you:

◆ Recognise the significant probability of sensory impairment?

◆ Assess and provide for mobility needs?

◆ Ensure access to help across client groups and teams?

◆ Offer opportunities for ordinary and specialist health services and therapies?

◆ Co-ordinate hospital admission and discharge with community services?

◆ Provide planned respite and crisis support services?

References

1. Roeher Institute. *Health Care.* Planning Innovations Project, 1994.
2. Smull M, Hamson S. Supporting people with severe reputations in the community. National Association of State Directors of Developmental Disabilities Services. Virginia, 1995.
3. Puddicombe B. *Face to Face. Communicating with people who do not use language.* Values into Action, 1995.
4. City & Hackney Community Services NHS Trust. Joint AAC Initiative. Final report of the Speech and Language Team, Learning Disabilities. June 1996 (unpublished document).
5. Emerson A. Facilitated communication: a practitioner's personal account. *Communication The National Autistic Journal* 1996; Spring:16–18.
6. Manthorpe J, Walsh M, Alaszewski A, Harrison L. Issues of risk practice and welfare in learning disability services. *Disability in Society Journal* 1997; 12(1):69-82.

7. *Planning for Life: Developing community services for people with complex multiple disabilities.* London: Department of Health and Social Services Inspectorate, 1995. No. 2 Good Practice in Manchester (1996). No. 3 Good Practice in the Independent Sector (1997).

Further reading

Fitton P. *Listen to Me: Communicating the needs of people with profound intellectual and multiple disabilities.* London: Jessica Kingsley, 1994.

Making It Happen. Community leisure and recreation for people with profound learning and multiple disabilities. Report and checklist. 1997. Available from: Mencap, 115 Golden Lane, London EC1Y 0TJ. Tel: 0171 454 0454.

Chapter 14

Health care in the community

Vision and Principles

Men and women with learning difficulties should benefit from all actions taken to improve the health of the whole population. They should have access to all health services, including health promotion and health education, programmes of health surveillance and maintenance, and primary and secondary health care, with appropriate additional support as required to meet individual need.

Guidance published in 1992[1] emphasised the continuing responsibility of health authorities to ensure that health care is provided for people with learning disabilities; general guidance to the health service, such as the *Patient's Charter,*[2] also applies to them.

Health authorities and GP fundholders must ensure that their contracts for health care have no gaps. Any problems in obtaining health care for people with learning disabilities should be identified and solutions found, and families and support services should help them to use the family doctor more actively.

Services for people with learning disabilities should focus clearly on the special risks to their health. Specifications for community teams, for instance, could include:

- promoting healthy lifestyles
- health promotion (e.g. diet, exercise and sexual health)
- detection of ill health by screening (e.g. thyroid disease in people with Down's Syndrome)
- providing support for people with learning disabilities and advice for staff to enable everyone to be included in health services offered to the whole population.[3] ■

Health promotion project

THE PROJECT WAS SET UP IN June 1996 as an alliance between Ealing, Hammersmith and Hounslow Health Authority (EHH HA), Riverside Mental Health Trust (RMHT), Services for People with Learning Disabilities and West London Health Promotion Agency (WLPHA).

The project focuses on enabling people with learning difficulties to develop healthier lifestyles by:

• training staff and carers;
• promoting access to physical activities programmes through local leisure opportunities in each borough;

• developing health alliances across services;
• developing a physical activity strategy;
• providing training on healthy eating and nutritional advice;
• improving access to GP and other primary care services. ■

Contact: Sue Denny, Riverside Mental Health Trust, Services for People with Learning Disabilities, 34 Galena Road, Hammersmith, London W6. Tel: 0181 846 6300. Stephen James, West London Health Promotion Agency. Tel: 0181 893 0100

The current scene

Recent government policy documents have set out clear guidelines and responsibilities for commissioners and providers about the planning and delivery of primary health care for men and women with learning difficulties. However, many people still receive a very poor service.

• People with learning difficulties experience the same range of health problems as the rest of the population yet tend to receive a worse service. For example, when visiting their GP, they are less likely to receive preventative health care such as immunisations and blood pressure checks compared with patients who don't have a learning difficulty.[4]

• They often have additional health care needs associated with their disability which go unrecognised. Some of the reasons for this are:
  – the masking of health problems by people's learning difficulties
  – their higher levels of physical and sensory impairment
  – low self-reporting of illness
  – a greater variety, number and frequency of health problems
  – a greater vulnerability to age-related physical and mental health problems
  – conservatism in determining whether people with learning difficulties can give consent to medical treatment.

• Communication problems also make it difficult for someone to describe symptoms or say how they feel.

- People who have lived in long-stay hospitals often don't have adequate medical records. Important information such as immunisation records, history of childhood diseases, history of seizures and drugs used are often missing.[5]

- GP fundholders and primary health care teams often feel uncertain about how to meet the health care needs of this group. They lack information about services available for them and are also concerned about obtaining adequate information, how to involve them in decisions and about the extra time needed. They are unsure about who has responsibility for service monitoring.[5]

Key points for future health care

Prescription for Change – A Mencap report on the role of GPs and carers in the provision of primary care to people with learning difficulties sets out key recommendations for the future[6]

- GPs should be the principal providers of primary medical care to people with learning difficulties

- Compulsory training for GPs in learning disability (medical and social issues) at under-graduate level and a greater availability of postgraduate refresher courses

- Improved training and information on health care issues for carers

- A co-ordinated approach to sharing information between primary health care teams and community learning disability teams which should be initiated by health authorities

- Social services departments should inform GPs of locally available services for people with learning difficulties

- All GPs should keep records which enable them to pick up special health communication needs of patients with a learning disability

- Development of patient-held health records to help in management across services and to promote user involvement

- Appropriate health screening for people with learning difficulties on an individual needs basis with accessible health promotion material

---

Personal health record

IN COLLABORATION WITH others, the National Development Team (NDT) has developed an easy-to-use personal health record for people with learning difficulties. This is a useful way to involve them in their own health care and reminds them of the importance of good health. ■

National Development Team. Advocating for Health: Your personal health record. *Available from: Harlow Print Ltd, Maxwell Street, South Shields, Tyne & Wear NE33 4PU. Tel: 0191 455 4286*

A better service for individuals

Planning and delivery of health care for people with learning difficulties should be constructed from the unique characteristics and needs of individuals and their families and each person's profile or lifeplan should include a section on this.

People with learning difficulties may have difficulty in recognising and describing symptoms of ill-health, particularly if they use only non-verbal communication. Staff need to be vigilant about recognising indications of pain or distress and keeping a detailed record of these signs for the benefit of staff and others who know the person less well.

Yearly health checks with the person's GP should be routine. Good use should also be made of Health Call, a domiciliary optical service free to people receiving benefits. (For further information see Chapter 13.)

When people visit their GP, it is important they receive appropriate support. Some will prefer to go on their own, but many will appreciate having someone along whom they choose and who knows them well. Those who use non-verbal communication will need to be equipped with appropriate signs, symbols, pictures or photographs to ensure they get their message across.

Registers

A sensitively handled register, taking careful account of confidentiality, dignity and respect can be used to provide a better service for people. Well-run registers, regularly updated, can ensure that people are sent relevant information about health care and collated information can be used to plan health and social care services.

Checklist for managers

◆ Establish flexibility with contracts and funding

◆ Ensure that each person with learning disabilities has a comprehensive annual health check

◆ Arrange regular screening to identify health problems and include hearing and eye tests

◆ Use the Personal Health Record to improve the involvement of individuals in their health care, prevent health problems and encourage healthy lifestyles: these can be ordered from Harlow Printing, Maxwell Street, South Shields, Tyne & Wear NE33 4PU. Tel: 0191 455 4286

◆ Include health promotion and identification of health problems in staff training.

◆ Help GPs and other primary health care staff to improve their communication skills using, for example, symbols and signs

◆ Co-ordinate working relationships between social services staff, primary health care teams and the community learning disability team with a focus on the individual

◆ Combine staff from the community learning disability teams and social services specialist staff to create one team with shared values

The community learning disability team

The role of the community learning disability team has changed since the introduction of care management and the transfer of many services to the independent sector. Their role is vital in the prevention, maintenance and delivery of health care and merging it with social care. An important feature of their work is to maintain communication with primary health care teams. However, a recent study reveals confusion about the roles and relationships between the two types of team. Communication and co-ordination with health care and social care professionals is under-developed. The role of the community learning disability team in providing specialist information, advice and support is unclear.[7]

The need for a multidisciplinary approach

A multidisciplinary approach where people with medical training, physiotherapists, occupational therapists, social workers and care managers are working together to common goals is absolutely essential. GPs need the input of these professionals to assist in effective planning and delivery of good health care.

Focus on Health Week

WEST SURREY HEALTH Authority organised a week of health related activities to raise awareness about people with learning difficulties and particularly about their health needs. The main aims of the week were:

- to promote greater awareness of the needs of people with learning difficulties particularly in relation to Health of the Nation key areas
- to offer advice and information on healthy lifestyles to people with learning difficulties and their carers

- to encourage communication, information and liaison between local agencies
- to provide information on leisure and social activities and offer opportunities to participate in activities at various venues
- to encourage communication between people with learning difficulties, carers and professionals

A full programme of events was organised on a wide variety of topics including personal safety, healthy eating, keep fit, sport, women's health, dance and movement, sexual health and stress management.

People with learning difficulties were actively involved in all aspects of organising, advertising and taking part in the week.

A paper on best practice locally and nationally was produced and a strategic framework for the health care of people with learning difficulties and their families and carers was developed. ■

Contact: Charles Micallef, Training and Information Officer, Health Promotion Service, West Surrey Health Authority, The White House, Crouch Oak Lane, Addleston, Surrey KT15 2AN. Tel: 01932 854476. Fax: 01932 828397.

Person-centred health care

A new model of health care planning and co-ordination is in the making. In the past, people with learning difficulties have often been excluded but as we move towards a social and human rights perspective, their inclusion must be a part of mainstream planning and decision-making. A new model must develop a multidisciplinary approach with a user focus. The planning process should affirm the central role of the person in shaping his/her own health care while recognising the importance of family and carers. This approach to planning and delivery of health care must not be divorced from the individual's own life goals and must maintain a commitment to enabling greater inclusion in the community.

References

1 *Health Care for People with Learning Difficulties (Mental Handicap).* HSG(92)42.

2. Department of Health. *The Patient's Charter.* London: Department of Health, 1991.

3. Department of Health. *Health of the Nation. A strategy for people with learning disabilities.* London: Department of Health, 1995.

4. Kerr MP, Richard D, Glover G. Primary care for people with intellectual disability: a group practice survey. *Bild Publication* 1996; 9(4):347–52.

5. Flynn M, Howard J, Pursey A. *GP Fund-Holding and the Health Care of People with Learning Difficulties.* Manchester: National Development Team, 1996.

6. Singh. *Prescription for Change: A Mencap report on the role of GPs and carers in the provision of primary care for people with learning difficulties.* Mencap Campaigns Department, June 1997.

7. Rimmer JW, Whitfield M. Can primary healthcare teams and community learning disability teams collaborate to provide preventative health care for patients with learning difficulties? *Audit Trends* 1996; 4(June):63–7.

Further reading and resources

Band R. *Getting Better: How people with learning difficulties can get the best from their GP. A video resource pack.*

Band R. *Keep Clean. Food. Safety in the Home.* Healthy living for people with learning difficulties. (Three booklets). Available from: The Access to Health Project. Elfrida Society, 34 Islington Park Street, London N1 1PX. Tel: 0171 359 7443; fax: 0171 704 1358.

Greenhalgh L. *Well Aware: Improving access to health information to people with learning difficulties.* London : NHS Executive, 1995. (Includes useful appendix on training materials).

Greig R, Peck E. Is there a future for the community learning disabilities team? *Tizard Learning Disability Review* 1998; 3(1).

Health Education Authority. *Health Related Resources for People with Learning Difficulties.* A directory which contains details of 160 nationally available health resources; reviews resources specifically for people with learning difficulties; and focuses on promoting health, healthy lifestyles and using health services. Available from: HEA Customer Services, Marston Book Services Limited, PO Box 269, Abingdon, Oxon OX14 4YN.

McRae D. Health care for women with learning disabilities. *Nursing Times* 1997; 93(15).

NHS Executive. *Signposts for Success: Commissioning and providing health services for people with learning disabilities. Summary of Signposts for Success. The Healthy Way.* London: NHS Executive, 1998.

Chapter 15

From hospital to community

Vision and Principles

Planning how men and women moving out of hospital will spend their daytime, evenings and weekends should begin at the same time as planning where they will live. This should start with a person-centred plan for each individual. Record past histories. Make use of the accumulated knowledge of staff who have known residents for many years but who may not be moving out with them.

Funding for day opportunities needs to be ring-fenced to prevent it being swallowed up as part of the residential contract with the provider.

Contracts should clearly specify the needs, wishes and goals for each person. Individualised contracts are a powerful and important way to achieve and maintain quality.

A continuous, cohesive training programme is important not only to develop skills but achieve attitude changes. Staff from all relevant organisations should be involved in order to break down professional and cultural barriers and promote common understanding. Arrange secondments to the community for hospital staff and to the hospital for people already working in the community.

An effective communication strategy with all stakeholders is vital. ■

The current scene

By 1993, places in long-stay hospitals in the UK had decreased by over 26,000. By the end of the century, at least 10,000 more men and women with learning difficulties in England alone will have moved out of hospital to live in the community. We are well down the road of closure but evidence from a variety of studies paints a mixed picture about the lives of people now living in the community.[1]

On the positive side, people:

- do enjoy a better material standard of living
- have more opportunities to use skills and develop new skills
- have more choice over routine daily activities
- have more contact with other people
- make more use of ordinary community facilities
- spend more time in constructive activities
- are relatively well accepted as customers in local businesses
- receive increased contact and support from care staff.

On the other hand, compared with the general population, they:

- remain relatively poor
- have few opportunities to make choices about life-defining decisions such as who to live with and who to be supported by
- have few relationships with non-disabled people other than care staff
- have little real presence in their community.

Overall, research has shown that people with learning disabilities, including those with more severe disabilities, can enjoy an improved standard of life in the community. However, services vary widely and a great deal depends on the quality of the support they receive.

The challenge for everyone involved in hospital resettlement programmes is to learn from past experience and strive to ensure that the positive outcomes of resettlement become commonplace.

With so little new money coming into services, the transfer of funding from long-stay hospitals into the community is one of the few opportunities to substantially redesign how people are supported. We must make the most of it and provide support through individualised financial arrangements and creative solutions such as setting up trusts which can be managed by a circle of support. (See 'A Circle of Support as a Trust', in Chapter 13.)

This chapter draws mainly on the lessons learned from working with Ely Hospital in Cardiff about day services change as part of a resettlement project, but also draws on experience from the other development sites and knowledge of good practice around the country generally.

Managing the culture gap

With hospital closure, responsibility for caring and supporting individuals often moves from health to social services or an independent voluntary sector organisation. This involves people from different backgrounds planning together and can result in clashes between organisational cultures. Keeping focused on the needs and wishes of individuals helps to overcome professional barriers, promote common understanding and a desire to work together towards the same goals.

Two new management posts at Ely Hospital – a planner and a line manager – helped bridge the gap between social services and health. These managers were based at the hospital although their background was in community social services and day services. While the going was not always easy, they helped to make things happen for individuals and played an important role in linking information from person-centred plans to strategic planning.

In addition, two members of staff from social services were seconded to the hospital to help plan new day opportunities. Bringing their considerable experience in day services into the hospital and encouraging hospital staff to communicate openly and share their ideas proved very successful. Good interpersonal skills, a facilitative approach and keeping the focus on good outcomes for residents, were crucial factors in ensuring the very effective contribution that these two people made.

Keeping person-centred

A hospital is a very complex place; it is difficult to be person-centred. In Ely Hospital, the following actions helped to maintain a person-centred approach and to focus on action to achieve changes in people's lives:

- Planning circles were set up involving paid and unpaid people to help each resident map out their future lifestyle. These were powerful tools towards achieving change.
- Funding devolved to ward managers made it easier to provide more varied experiences in the community. Previous administrative procedures like excessive form-filling or the petty cash office not opening at weekends made this difficult and discouraged staff from making the effort. One ward pooled residents' mobility allowance to lease a vehicle. Through measures such as these, spontaneous arrangements became possible and staff had the satisfaction of not only hearing what the person wanted to do but making it happen.
- Continuous staff development. Secondments to progressive community-based organisations helped staff see new possibilities for individuals and different ways of working.

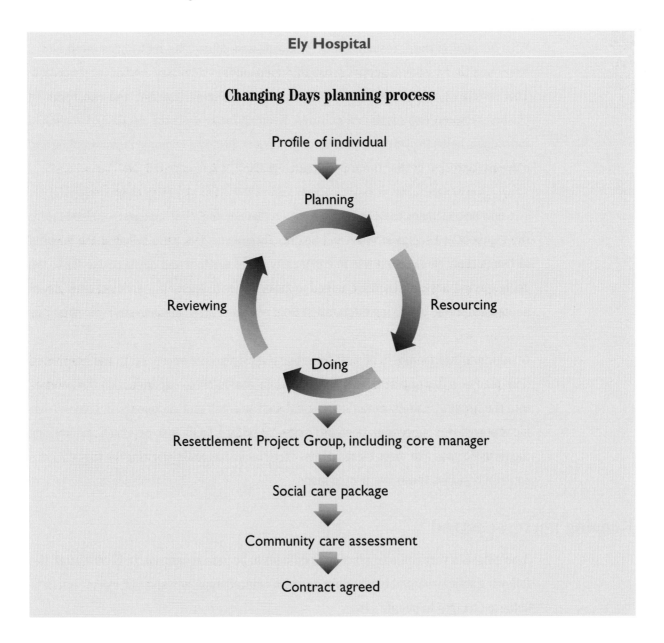

Ely Hospital

Changing Days planning process

Profile of individual

Planning

Reviewing   Resourcing

Doing

Resettlement Project Group, including core manager

Social care package

Community care assessment

Contract agreed

The profiling process

Creating an effective profile for each person is a crucial first step towards achieving a better quality of life for them when they leave hospital. It should examine all aspects of their lives, including where they wish to live, who they wish to live with, how they wish to spend their days, their health care needs and the levels of support they require. Everyone who knows the person should be involved. It is important to include ward staff as they usually have great knowledge about the individual which is often not recorded. (See Chapter 7.)

However, in the resettlement situation, the problems caused by hospital closure can overwhelm the creation of a process based on individual needs. Staff fears about their future, negative attitudes towards the closure, the personal investment many staff have made in the hospital over many years, the complex hospital culture built up over a long period – all combine to dampen innovation. Staff may already be struggling with lack of resources, reduced staffing, closing wards, and a general sense of everything grinding to a halt. To be asked, therefore, to complete profiles will seem like extra work in an already over-stressed environment.

To overcome some of these problems, Ely Hospital appointed additional staff on short-term contracts to work with ward staff. Lessons learned from this were:

- staff need to respect and recognise each other's skills and backgrounds, be good listeners and teamworkers
- both 'old' and 'new' staff need to share innovative opportunities (e.g. taking people out to try new activities in the community) as well as more routine tasks (e.g. covering for other staff on ward duties)
- the profiling process needs to be clear and easily understood by everyone involved. People need to understand why the profile is necessary, where it fits into the planning process and be confident it will be acted upon
- the forms used to create the profile should not only be person-centred and comprehensive but should be easy to complete. (See examples in Appendix.)

Planning Circles
The process

Planning Circles proved to be a valuable method of gathering information. From this a formal process was devised with the Changing Days co-ordinator to fit in with the resettlement process and the hospital.

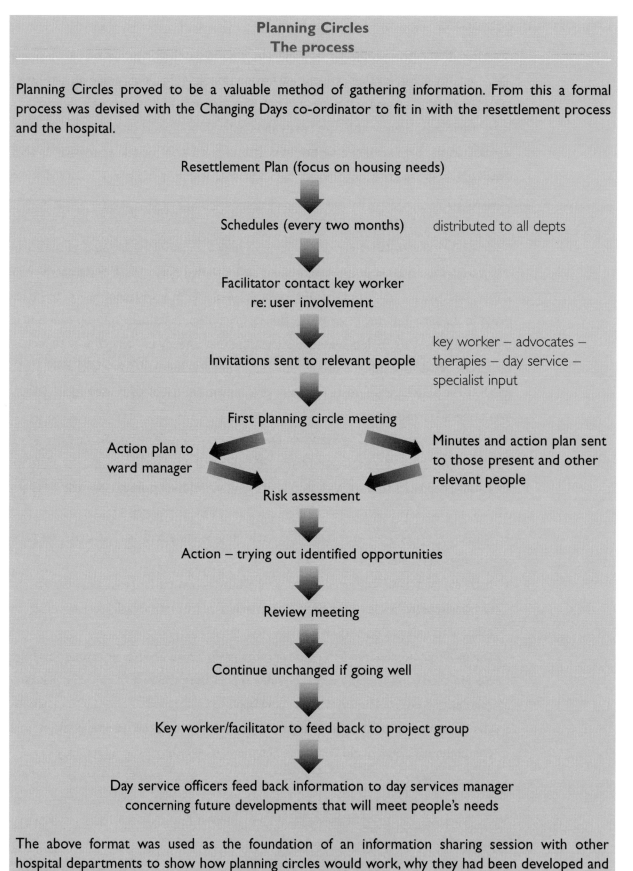

Resettlement Plan (focus on housing needs)

Schedules (every two months)   distributed to all depts

Facilitator contact key worker
re: user involvement

Invitations sent to relevant people   key worker – advocates –
therapies – day service –
specialist input

First planning circle meeting

Action plan to   Minutes and action plan sent
ward manager   to those present and other
relevant people

Risk assessment

Action – trying out identified opportunities

Review meeting

Continue unchanged if going well

Key worker/facilitator to feed back to project group

Day service officers feed back information to day services manager
concerning future developments that will meet people's needs

The above format was used as the foundation of an information sharing session with other hospital departments to show how planning circles would work, why they had been developed and how they would fit into the resettlement process and beyond.

A first circle

I had my first Planning Circle meeting in May. There were lots of people there who I knew. They were asking what I wanted to do with my time.

I told them that I like to be busy and that most of all I'd like a job as a security guard but I know that jobs are hard to come by. I also told them that I'd like to:

- learn how to use a computer
- learn how to manage my money a bit better
- go to pottery classes, art classes and photography classes.

In my spare time I said that I'd like to:

- go bike riding
- play football
- go to watch Barry Town football matches
- do outdoor pursuits like walking, camping, climbing, abseiling and caving.

Unfortunately, none of these things has happened yet, but I've been told that I'm starting outdoor pursuits tomorrow. I think that's wonderful and I'm looking forward to it.

Mike Hookings, former resident, Ely Hospital

Recording past life history

Enormous amounts of information about people's lives – their family backgrounds, who they are and what they are like as individuals – are lost when they leave hospital. Often, there are few photographs except recent holiday snaps. Not enough importance is given to recording information that staff may possess about residents they have known for many years.

Some people will be reluctant to pass on negative information about the person or their history. They will argue for the chance to start with a clean sheet, or show concern about confidentiality with regard to family history. This is wholly understandable but should not be used as a blanket excuse. For example, families who lost touch years earlier and who may initially be hostile to the idea of renewing contact, can change when the person is living a different lifestyle.

This area needs sensitive handling to ensure that no information which may help to re-connect people or reconstruct a life history is lost. Our past is a vital part of who we are and can provide valuable clues to help shape a new life in the community.

The day opportunities worker

In Cambridge, a number of young people with high support needs who used to live in Ida Darwin Hospital are now living in average sized bungalows and going out each day to varied activities in the community. Day opportunity staff who have expertise in developing community opportunities work alongside residential workers. Segregated situations are avoided and wherever possible people join in activities alongside ordinary people living in the community. Developing relationships with the general public is the major challenge for staff in these circumstances.

The role of care management

Care managers who are seconded to work from a hospital are well positioned to smooth the path into the community. Their aim is to purchase individualised opportunities for people and to link plans for their daytime with the rest of their community care assessment.

Parents and carers

Working closely with parents and carers is vital. (See Chapter 9.) Many men and women living in hospital have few or no links with their families. In these instances, it is particularly important to record any information – even distant memories – which staff and other people in the hospital may have about the person's family or background. Sensitive exploration of this area after people are settled in their new home may lead to renewed contact with family. Such links are a good base from which to start reconnecting people with the outside world.

Reference

1. Emerson E, Hatton C. *Moving Out: Relocation from hospital to community.* Manchester: Hester Adrian Research Centre, 1994.

A parent's view

On Monday 13 January 1975, I conceded defeat and took my two sons, P and R, to be admitted into hospital. After ten unhappy, troublesome years they were transferred to another hospital. As the boys grew older, their behaviour problems increased. Home visits became a weekly nightmare. Neither wanted to return to hospital and R, in particular, would bang the car windows once he realised we were on the return journey. I believe he was showing his frustration and distress in the only way open to him. I love my children dearly, but that love was sorely tested and then the feelings of guilt would take over. I could not ignore their existence but seeing them was causing fresh grief every week to all the family.

When the possibility of resettlement was put to me, my reactions were varied and, if I am honest, negative. I was worried about funding, about support and about neighbourhood reactions. I also felt guilty – were those years in hospital unnecessary?

Now both P and R are living in their own homes. I was involved with the planning at every stage – their individual profiles, interviews for the staff, selecting furniture and fittings for the houses.

Both are extremely happy and leading full and rich lives. P still enjoys coming out in the car, but is always happy to return – signing 'home' to convey his meaning. R is less eager to come out, I think he worries I will return him to hospital. I am invited in for a cup of coffee, then shown the door with a hug and a wave.

Yes, I still have worries, but what mother doesn't? I am learning to put my concerns into perspective. P and R are thoroughly enjoying their new life. God and Government willing, it will continue for the rest of their lives. Nobody should be committed to a hospital ward just because they are born less able.

✓ Checklist for managers

◆ Day services must be on the resettlement agenda from the beginning.

◆ Make sure that day service specialists are on the resettlement team.

◆ Set up a day service team within the hospital. This helps day services staff to get to know and work with the hospital culture and residents' experiences and promotes collaborative working between health and social services.

◆ Give the resettlement team a budget they can use to pilot innovative ideas and respond to information from the person-centred plans. The Ely Hospital team had about £20,000 a year which led to an arts agency, job coaching, travel training and a sports and leisure development officer.

◆ Community businesses and employment should be central to any resettlement process. Level of disability is no indicator of employability. With the right amount of support to both employer and employee even men and women with high support needs can secure jobs.

◆ The planning process should be co-ordinated across all departments. It should be comprehensive and include all aspects of a person's life.

◆ Share important information from the person-centred plans early on with colleges, mainstream leisure departments and other community-based services in order to make sure they will be able to include people from the hospital.

◆ Use circles of support or planning circles to bring together a range of individuals who know the person and who can really make things happen. These circles should continue after the person has left hospital. This is important for continuity and quality, but perhaps even more, for fostering friendships and building long-standing relationships which are so under-developed for most men and women living in hospitals.

◆ Maintain staffing levels and quality in supporting individuals who are still living in hospital. Many staff will find new jobs before the hospital closes. Flexible terms and conditions to bring in staff to cover these gaps are vital to maintain the quality of support to individuals.

◆ Arrange training for hospital staff in the social and developmental model of disability, not only to help them support people moving out in the community but to improve their own chances of employment in the new services.

◆ Match the interests of people who live in hospital with those of staff to help people participate in ordinary activities. Sharing interests and hobbies is a pleasurable way to try out new activities.

◆ Enable workers in residential homes to straddle the role of residential and day service worker.

◆ Arrange open days for hospital staff and residents to increase knowledge of the range of community opportunities available.

◆ Appoint community access officers to develop ordinary opportunities. (See Chapter 6)

◆ Invest in advocacy. People First and other forms of user empowerment are an essential part of shifting the culture away from institutional care.

◆ Produce a regular newsletter about what and where things are happening. Include hospital residents on its editorial board.

Chapter 16

Finance

Vision and Principles

New-style day services require radical new thinking about financial systems, costing and allocating resources.

The role of the statutory services will look very different and will revolve around three activities – person-centred planning, personal support, and community bridge-building. This will require major change in the way finance is organised and used.

There is no magic financial formula to help us move from the present system to a new service. The challenge is to find such a radically new approach that financial modelling as it is today becomes a fiscal museum piece. ■

Using current resources differently

One of the barriers to change most frequently cited by those connected to existing day services is the difficulty of releasing money from the current service to re-invest in a new one. Whatever else you may try, every morning large numbers of people arrive in buses and taxis at a building: the building eats up money, transport eats up money, and keeping people occupied eats up time and money. You cannot simply stop all this in one day.

The problem is compounded by the fact that although there are many examples of innovative daytime opportunities, most of them have been funded with 'new' money or money earmarked for people leaving hospital. We have also learned that there are ways to design and co-ordinate 'packages' for individuals, rather than seek funding for a whole service: the Andover Care Management Project in Hampshire was doing this in 1990.[1] For a time it seemed that care management might be the answer: give care managers the budget, and they would decide what to buy for individuals. This would become a finance-led way to change what people got. But these projects and innovations have worked only for a few.

So we are still stuck with the problem of how to release the large sums of money committed to centre-based services. This is felt more keenly of course as access to new money becomes more and more difficult, with the result that continuous funding for many innovative schemes is threatened. Proven alternatives like supported employment seem to hit a funding plateau.

Perhaps the mistake has been to believe there was some magic formula by which we could move from the existing service model to a new one – that is, identify existing costs, assess need and then calculate the costs of the new service. Such an approach is similar to that used in most hospital resettlement projects. These have ended up with a new service model that probably costs more (particularly if the social security benefits are included in the calculation) and is felt to have many of the problems of the older service model.

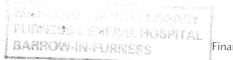

The old paradigm

Residential services: £ Local Authority   £ Health

| HOSPITAL | → | HOSTEL | → | GROUP HOME – ? |
| ATC | → | SEC | → | RESOURCE CENTRE – ? |

Day services: £ Local Authority   £ Health

That is the old paradigm and we know it does not work – or at least it just creates a new institutionalised approach along the same path as before. This book is about a new paradigm that challenges all the old assumptions about simply moving from one service model to another. The challenge for services is to think themselves into a new approach where current conventional financial modelling is difficult to imagine.

The new paradigm

Person-centred planning

↓

Advocacy

↓

Social inclusion

↓

Inclusive communities

The implications for services are far-reaching. It is not simply replacing one box with a lump of money attached to it (day services) with a number of smaller boxes using the same lump of money. It is about using all the money currently invested in health and local authority services and combining this with all the resources that will be required from elsewhere – benefits, wages, education, housing, leisure and so on – to create and support individual lifestyles for people. And because individual lifestyles can be complex, can change, and require creativity and flexibility, the business of costing this is difficult and uncertain.

What we do know is that the statutory service will look completely different and will revolve around three activities – person-centred planning, personal support and community bridge-building.

A new statutory service

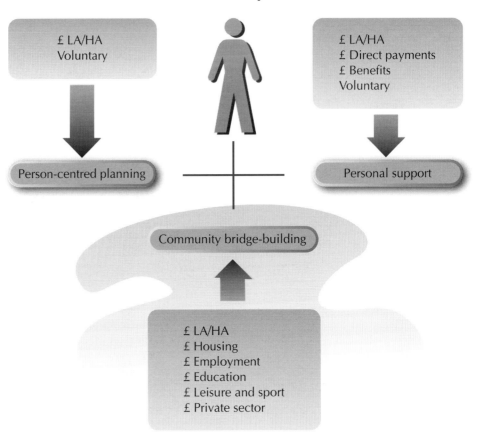

A new statutory service: resources

- *Investment in staff to learn about, lead and co-ordinate person-centred planning.* Staff do not have to be care managers, although their involvement may be necessary to access resources. If care managers do it, it must be recognised as different from the care management process. The responsibility for leading and co-ordinating this process, and therefore the cost, is likely to fall on health or social services initially. However, staff from other agencies and volunteers (family, friends, advocates) may be involved as the aim of person-centred planning is to include those people most important to the person at the centre of it.

- *Access to variable levels of appropriate personal support.* The amount and type of support will depend on the individual's needs and is likely, therefore, to vary enormously from person to person. Such money could come from a variety of sources – statutory agencies, independent support agencies, volunteers, advocates, friends or family. The cost would fall principally on the statutory agencies, but might also be supplemented by benefit income and the voluntary contribution of other people's time. Use of direct payments provides the opportunity to start using some of the statutory resources for individuals to purchase their own personal support needs. (See annex to this chapter for summary.)

- *Investment in 'community bridge-building'.* That is, specialist staff with skills to create, enable or develop access to a range of community resources in all 'life's domains' – education, training, work, leisure, sport. These bridge-building resources may be paid for by health or social services, but could come from other public service agencies, such as education, housing and leisure services; or from public funding sources, such as the European Social Fund and Training and Enterprise Councils. Money could also come from the private sector.

The lesson from small-scale innovative person-centred planning projects is that separate resources are required for bridge-building. A good illustration of this is supported employment. Supported employment services help with finding jobs, making effective job placements, and providing good on-the-job training and support and require a dedicated service with specific skills. This is additional to the wider person-centred planning and more immediate personal supports an individual will need. However, some supported employment schemes find themselves doing everything, usually because no one else is doing it. This unfortunately ties up specialist skills. More appropriately, an effective person-centred planning service would look after personal support not related to employment.

The complexities of diverse spending

The funding of supported employment agencies is not straightforward. Many started with financial backing from social services and health authorities, but this has often been short term. The question arises: why should health and social care money pay for employment? Is this not someone else's responsibility? Some have had money from TECs or other employment sources (particularly the European Social Fund, although this is only 'matched funding'), but the issue here is lack of understanding of the particular employment needs – and potential – of people traditionally classified as 'incapable of work' by the employment and benefit system.

Government policy now accepts the right to work for all. The Employment Service already operates the Access to Work scheme which recognises supported employment and the present Labour Government has included people with learning difficulties in the Welfare to Work scheme. There are still barriers – loss of entitlement to benefits, arbitrary cut-off points between earned income and benefits – but there is a definite trend to reduce dependency on welfare by employment initiatives, and people with learning difficulties can benefit from this if they are made aware of it, and opportunities taken.

Similar issues are replicated wherever the new paradigm pushes people towards the concept of inclusion in all aspects of life. Money to enable inclusion and strengthen it may come from many and different sources, and will need to be separately fought for by people with proper skills. There are many examples: leisure and recreation departments providing development officers; sports associations providing specialist staff; further education providing personal support to students; leisure link schemes and community access officers.

Implications of the new paradigm for funding strategic change

- Current day services cannot be looked at in isolation, nor their funding. Consideration of someone's whole life requires abandoning the old boundaries of residential and day services and using the combined resources to develop better opportunities for them.
- Investment will need to be made in an infrastructure of person-centred planning and community bridge-building. Beyond these, funding for individual support will be bespoke and infinitely variable.
- The sources of both financial and non-financial support will be diverse and complex, hard to define and variable across localities.
- Strong partnerships with all relevant agencies and sectors in all localities should make best use of resources. But not if those are simply cost-shunting exercises: housing,

leisure, and other services must help but only as partners, getting the expert assistance they need from health and social care agencies.

- Strategies that help people make the most of their own income will be better for that individual, and could reduce agencies' costs. This means giving priority to work opportunities and expert benefit advice and support.
- It will be very difficult to cost the 'new service' and is therefore important to define:
  – who the service is for: the numbers and the eligibility criteria
  – the total health and social services resources available
  – the potential contribution from other sources towards infrastructure costs
  – defining the resources available for the person-centred planning process itself
  – defining the level of investment in community bridge-building.

With simple care management assessment, it may be possible to 'band' resources to pay for support based on different levels of eligibility. This would provide statutory resource parameters for individuals within the person-centred planning process to maximise other inputs for that person.

- Implementation will be slow and in stages. There is no instant replacement for the existing service. But there needs to be a strategy that starts the new process for a few people and is then able to claw back money from the existing service as more people develop other options for their lives.

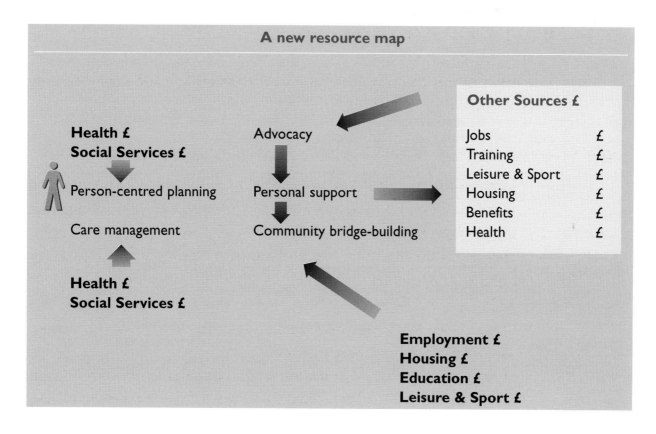

A new resource map

Health £
Social Services £

Person-centred planning

Care management

Health £
Social Services £

Advocacy

Personal support

Community bridge-building

Other Sources £

Jobs   £
Training   £
Leisure & Sport £
Housing   £
Benefits   £
Health   £

Employment £
Housing £
Education £
Leisure & Sport £

Using money differently

One day centre officer post converted into revenue may give as many as 30 service users £500 a year to spend; that amount of money can open up a whole new world of access to community services. For instance, a mainstream adult education class may cost £2 per session; ten individuals studying different subjects in a general public class would cost approximately the same as one worker at the centre. The benefit to the ten could be immense, while no detrimental effect to staffing levels should be experienced providing these individuals can follow these courses without professional support.

This principle becomes harder to invoke the higher or more specialised a person's support needs are. However, for possibly 20 per cent of most people attending centres, it is an entirely realistic and relatively simple proposition, although it takes a brave and confident manager to implement.

Kingsthorpe Lighthouse

Cambridgeshire Social Services

THE CREATION OF THE Lighthouse was one of those rare moments in large organisations when, for a few, service development exactly matches people's needs at that particular moment.

It all started when, for various different reasons, a small number of people found themselves together at a large multi-purpose day centre. Some had spent up to twenty years at a local adult training centre. Others, due to difficulties in their personal life, had been placed at the centre because no other more suitable resource had been available. It was clear that although these people had very different aspirations and skills, they were linked by a common thread of boredom with the existing service.

To begin changing this situation, two crucial decisions were made. The first was to assign a half-time worker to work only with these individuals. The second was to renegotiate the cleaning contract at the centre to gain approximately £4,000 for the group to do with as they wished.

For the first six months the worker concentrated *only* on supporting people to develop skills in areas which were directly useful in general community life, such as lateral thinking, problem-solving, making choices, building relationships. During this period, the worker also focused on supporting families and carers. In fact, one third of the time was spent in this activity and this intensive input resulted in families remaining consistently supportive even though at times it was extremely difficult emotionally.

People were soon spending more and more time away from the centre accessing on their own a whole range of activities which no professional could ever have imagined. The money mentioned above had been divided to give each person £500 per year. It was also clear that the Centre as a base was becoming a major hindrance and so a bungalow belonging to the department in the city centre was gained and then furnished using slippage from the staffing budget.

One-and-a-half full-time equivalent staff members now support over thirty people from The Lighthouse. Many people from the original group are now living in their own homes and several have formed long-term relationships.

The cost to the department is approximately £1,200 per year per person, which is about one third of the original placement cost at the day centre. ■

Direct payments

Let me tell you about how my life has changed over the last few years thanks to receiving direct payments.

In early 1995, it was clear that my disability was preventing me from doing the things I really wanted to do, which was to continue to live independently, continue to work, and have control of my life. I needed a support worker. At the time, I was told that the only help I could have was home care, which would consist of a woman (no men apply for such employment) calling each morning to assist me to shower, get dressed, and have breakfast. This did not help me get out of the house into the community, go swimming, go shopping for clothes, etc. As I was faced with a 'take it or leave it' decision, I wrote a complaint to social services, advising them that the service I was being offered did not meet my needs. Then after several meetings with social services, it was agreed that I could employ my own care worker.

It was clear from the start that Luke and I would get on. It's important that you choose an assistant who likes doing the things you do. There were many things I wanted to do before Luke was employed. So at his interview I made it clear that I expected him not just to help get me up and dressed in the mornings but to also keep me active during the day by taking me out swimming, walking, to the doctor and dentist; help me get into my parents' house, so I could sit in the garden in the summer. He loves it, sitting in the garden, going for a swim, shopping and getting paid for it. It sounds great, but all the time he is working and doing the things I want to do and am unable to do without his help.

By employing my own assistant I'm part of the community and can get involved in activities like fund-raising and supporting my local workers to save their jobs. I don't sit behind closed doors hidden from everyone. The people who live in my neighbourhood are more aware of my needs because they see how Luke is helping me. We go swimming when I choose, and when it fits in with my schedule. Before I used to have to wait for one of my brothers to finish work and take me. The pool would always be busy and I wouldn't be able to swim properly. Now when I go it's in the afternoon before the pool gets busy, I can swim easily and Luke can give me some physiotherapy in the water.

cont.

Everyone's needs are different, so it's important that before you interview someone you have a clear idea what you want them to do. Start by writing down what your needs are. Don't be afraid to ask someone to help you, a friend or a member of your family or your social worker. Begin from getting up in the morning and go through your daily routine, make sure your day is planned on things you really want to do and like doing, all of which should be part of your community care assessment. Once you have your daily plan, and the amount of assistance has been agreed with your social services, it's time to start looking for your assistant.

Gary Nield

Brief summary on direct payments

- No additional funding is available to local authorities.

- Direct payments are only to be made to pay for the community care service that a person has been assessed as needing.

- The person must be over the age of 18 and under 65 at the start of receiving direct payment, but if direct payments begin before 65, they can continue after 65.

- Social service departments are given the power to make direct payments. It is not a duty to do so. They can also provide a mixture of direct payments and some services.

- Only social services have been given the power to make direct payments. Health authorities and housing departments cannot make direct payments.

- Direct payments cannot be used to purchase health authority or housing department services.

- They cannot be used to substitute permanent residential care, but can be used to pay for short-term residential care. However, there are time limits on the amount of residential care you can purchase.

- Local authorities can refuse to make direct payments to any person they feel cannot manage. However, people may obtain the support of others providing that they retain ultimate control over how the money is spent.

- A third party can receive the fund on behalf of the person receiving direct payments. Provided the person remains in control. It's therefore possible for people to employ a payroll service, for example, to assist with PAYE and NIC.

- It is not possible for people in receipt of direct payments to pay for a service provided by a relative, e.g. mother, father, brother.

cont.

- Once in receipt of direct payments a person must ensure that proper records of how the money is spent are kept, and also that should there be a breakdown in the normal service, i.e. the person they employ cannot work, they can call upon a backup to ensure they still receive the help they need.

- Direct payments can also be made to people to purchase aids and adaptations provided that the aid comes under the legal definition of community care service or would otherwise be provided by the social services department.

- Direct payments can be stopped by the recipient or social services at any time.

Assessing the user's ability to manage

- Does the person understand the nature of direct payments?
- Can the person express preferences (with assistant to communicate their view, if necessary) between different types of service?
- Does the person currently take other important decisions for himself or herself?
- Will the person be able to keep the necessary records?
- Does the person understand the legal responsibilities that may arise if he or she becomes an employer, and can he or she cope with them?
- Will the person be able to ensure that he or she receives services he or she has paid for?
- Is the person likely to be able to manage direct payments on an ongoing basis, as opposed to having a fluctuating or deteriorating condition which may affect his or her ability to manage?

If the answer to either of the first two questions is 'no' then the person is unlikely to be able to manage direct payments. A negative answer to the remaining questions may also raise doubts.

A person can receive assistance with managing direct payments, and where they do not have access to help the local authority may offer training to enable them to manage.

Source: Abstracted from Department of Health. *Community Care (Direct Payments) Act 1996: Policy and practice guidance.* London: DoH, 1997.

References

1. Archer R, Robinson G. *The Andover Case Management Project: Services for people with a mental handicap.* Winchester: Winchester DHA, 1990.
2. Wright K. Community care (direct payments). *Llais* 1997; 47(Winter):17–20.

Further reading

Joseph Rowntree Foundation. *Direct Payment for People with Learning Difficulties.* York: Joseph Rowntree Foundation, 1997.

Chapter 17

Staff development

Visions and Principles

A day service which realises the potential of its staff will:

- find ways of involving them in redesigning the service to better meet people's needs;
- support them in coming to terms with the change in role this will entail;
- enable them to learn the necessary skills the new service demands;
- support them in putting these new skills into practice;
- help them to draw on their individual skills, interests and aspirations.

(Changing Days, 1996)

The health of the organisation and the quality of the service delivered will depend considerably on the learning and development of its main resource: the staff. (Sawden, 1995)

Effective training is the cornerstone of successful organisational change and, without it, lasting change to the culture and ethos of that organisation is unlikely to be achieved. Training which also inspires is vital.

- How can training support the process of changing culture and values?
- What should a training strategy consist of?
- How do you assess the training needs of staff?
- How can service users and carers be included in training?
- What are the different approaches to training?
- How do you know if training has been successful?

This chapter explores these questions. ■

The wrong sort of training

Training is all right but some of the time I sit in training wondering what else I could be getting on with if I hadn't been forced to come. The trouble is that some of the training I go to doesn't seem to have any relevance to my work, or it's telling me things I already know, or it's too simplistic, or the trainer knows less about the subject than I do, or we spend so much time in groups putting the world to rights that we never get round to taking any action. Worst of all is the endless writing on flipcharts which, after the event, no one ever sees again. Some of my best doodles have been done during training events. I have a collection of them at work.

A disgruntled participant, July 1997

The role of training in the change process

Training is often seen by participants as a safe environment in which to express views and concerns. Certainly it is often easier to discuss and resolve controversial issues in such an environment rather than in a meeting. Training events are often held away from the workplace and participants may feel less inhibited. People may be more open to new ideas than if presented with them in a formal meeting. Training is thus a good opportunity to discuss and agree change. In addition, new ideas and philosophies presented in training make the acceptance of new values and the need to change culture seem more reasonable. Training can help to relieve the stress of change for all concerned.

✓ Checklist

- ◆ Be clear about why training is necessary
- ◆ Make sure you know what you want training to achieve
- ◆ Don't isolate training from the rest of the change process
- ◆ Choose your venue with care. The right venue can contribute to the success of the event
- ◆ Remember that training and education are different things. People will often accept a need to change values and attitudes if they have been educated to understand why they should change rather than be told when they should change.
- ◆ Design and advertise the training in a way that makes people want to attend and participate.
- ◆ Explain the relevance of particular pieces of training to staff's work. Training people who have been forced to attend is often a waste of time

Developing the training strategy

Any training strategy is only as good as the skills of the people who deliver it. However, there are some fundamental points that should be taken into consideration. Training must be part of the overall policy for change. It is not good enough to limit discussion of it to one paragraph buried in the middle of the key policy document. Neither is it sensible to have a training strategy but no policy to train for. Training and change policy must go hand in hand.

You must identify who needs to be trained and why, what the organisation, staff, users and carers should get out of it and how long training should last. For example, in the context of changing days, the organisation needs staff who are good networkers, confident risk-takers, who enjoy working independently and who are well connected within their local community. Staff may also require assertiveness skills, time management skills and opportunities to share individual ideas about how to create new day opportunities. Service users may need training in how best to communicate the kind of day opportunities they might enjoy. And carers may need training in how to manage direct care payments or obtain the best from review meetings. The training strategy must be comprehensive enough to incorporate a wide range of needs, but it must also be flexible and adapt to opportunities or obstacles that may arise.

Things to include in a training strategy

- The purpose of the strategy
- Why it is needed
- How the strategy links with other things going on in the organisation
- What it aims to achieve
- Who the strategy is about: staff, service users, carers, managers, other organisations
- Who will be involved in implementing the strategy
- How long will it last
- How much will it cost
- What types of training will be included and why
- How the strategy will be monitored and evaluated
- What opportunities will there be to alter it if necessary
- Who has been involved in writing the strategy
- What the intended outcomes are

> ### ✓ Checklist
>
> ◆ Make sure that the training strategy is part of, or reflects, the values and objectives of the whole change process
>
> ◆ Don't take it for granted that everyone will view training as important or necessary in order to effect change
>
> ◆ Review the training strategy regularly
>
> ◆ Don't give total responsibility for the training to the trainers. Remain involved with the training programme. Go along to training events to show staff, service users and carers that you are committed to change too
>
> ◆ Avoid the outcomes noted in the case study by ensuring that participants can see how aspects of training form part of the overall scheme

One person must lead the training programme, but the responsibility for its content belongs to everyone. Before writing a training strategy make sure you consult as many people as possible. If it is to succeed, it must balance the needs of all stakeholders. Everyone needs to feel they will gain from it.

> ### ✓ Checklist
>
> ◆ Don't assume everyone has the same training needs
>
> ◆ Don't assume that the same method of training will be right for everyone
>
> ◆ Make it everyone's responsibility to identify training needs and how they might be met
>
> ◆ Where possible, link training to National Vocational Qualifications or other professional awards such as post-basic nursing or social work qualifications
>
> ◆ Don't assume that every training need can be met only by an expert
>
> ◆ Avoid the outcomes noted in the case study by ensuring that each piece of training operates at a variety of levels. For example, staff with very different levels of understanding can attend the same course but learn at different levels of complexity by the way you structure your presentations and group work

Identify the training needs of staff

If you attempt to identify training needs of staff without consultation, you may well end up teaching them what they already know. Identifying their training needs in the context of change must also take account of their career development plans or wishes regarding achievement of professional qualifications. Begin by brainstorming all the skills you may need before and after change has taken place. Ask people what they think their training needs are. Send out questionnaires, attend staff meetings, and ask service users. Make the business of identifying training needs a continuous process. Don't assume that one training course will meet all the requirements of everyone. Try to link training needs to those of service users as well as the local communities where staff will be working. For example, if public transport is poor and staff are unhappy about driving themselves, send them on a course designed to improve driving skills and confidence.

Include service users and carers

Enabling service users and carers to attend and participate in training events is not always easy. For instance, trainers may not know any service users or carers. Staff may be embarrassed sharing personal concerns about their jobs with service users and carers. However, if such events are a safe place for staff to raise concerns, they may also be a safe place for service users and carers to talk openly.

When providing training for service users or carers it may be necessary to run courses in the evenings or at weekends. Get their names and addresses from staff and send them details through the post. In addition, it may be necessary for trainers to visit service users and carers to explain why they might find the training on offer useful.

Service users and carers also have an important role in the overall training process. They can help staff and other carers and users understand the reasons for change. They can be champions of change and often take the process further than was originally anticipated.

Checklist

◆ Make sure service users and carers are included in all training offered wherever possible

◆ Make sure that training does not include a chosen few service users and carers at the expense of the many

◆ Avoid the outcomes noted in the case study by recognising that everyone who attends a training event brings their own skills, knowledge and experience. Remember and tell participants that you, the trainer, don't know everything. You can learn as much from them as they can learn from you

Choose an appropriate format

There are four core elements for training: the conference format, the short-course format, the workshop format and the briefing session.

Holding a conference is one way of beginning and ending a process of change. It is a useful method for presenting the reasons for change to the widest audience. However, it does have a drawback because it's difficult to tell if everyone agrees with the subjects under discussion as most people find it hard to contribute in a large group.

The short-course format is useful as an aid to team development or for re-skilling people who need to change their work practices. For example, if staff currently employed in two different day centres are moving to a shared community base it might be useful to set up a series of training sessions that give them an opportunity to learn new skills and get to know one another.

The workshop format has many purposes. A one- or two-day workshop might be the focus for specific 'project planning', 'team development' or 'skill development'. Project planning in a workshop enables people to work without the normal distractions of office life. Project planning workshops are useful for inter-agency planning. Team development workshops are a way of helping people come to terms with change. Include the whole team when planning team development and make the programme explicit so that people don't come wondering whether there is a hidden agenda. Skill development workshops take many forms. For example, they may cover a specific subject such as sexuality. Don't assume that the knowledge to run a workshop does not exist locally. In return for the latest literature a local practitioner may well be prepared and competent enough to run a workshop.

The briefing session is the best way to communicate how changes are progressing or to seek comments on particular issues. In a briefing session the same information can be shared with different groups in different ways. For example, as part of changing days it is important to discuss how people feel about the move from buildings-based services to community-based services, but senior managers may prefer to debate the issues in a different way to service users or front-line staff. Whichever format you select, it is important to ensure that each event is not seen in isolation from other training. For example, if you are running two workshops on the implications of changing days for service users, one for managers and one for day centre officers, the presentation part of the workshop should be the same, although the group work might be different to reflect the particular issues that their status requires them to consider.

✓ Checklist

- ◆ Choose the format for your events with care. Depending on the required outcome the format can have a significant bearing on your success
- ◆ Be prepared to do the same piece of training in different formats depending on the audience
- ◆ Use a format that is appropriate to your audience and the type of material you wish to present. Don't run an event with too little or too much material: participants can go away feeling they have wasted time because there wasn't enough to do or you may inadvertently omit the very material that is of use to them

Make time for evaluation

Successful training is not about the number of people who turned up. Neither is it to be judged on the number of people who ticked 'very happy' on the evaluation forms. Finding out whether a training event or series of events worked takes time. Time for evaluation needs to be part of the training strategy.

As well as overall aims for the training strategy, make sure that each event has aims which can be understood by those who take part. If a training event is to be repeated, contact those who have already participated and ask if it helped them change their practice.

Look for unexpected effects it may have had. Be prepared to rewrite your material based on feedback. However, don't automatically call for a rewrite every time a training course appears to be poorly received. People sometimes come to training courses with false expectations or a lack of understanding about the content. Sometimes they will say it was no good because they do not want to change their practice.

Finally, make sure there is good communication between trainers and managers at all times. Without this, training can sometimes get separated from the process of change and trainers and managers can, if you are not careful, end up contradicting each other, thus making staff, service users and carers confused and defensive about the whole issue.

✓ Checklist

- ◆ Be clear about your definition of success before the training starts
- ◆ Don't regard a training event as successful just because everyone turned up
- ◆ Be prepared to talk to people days or even weeks after a training event to find out which parts really made a difference to their lives
- ◆ Ensure you maintain good communication links between managers and trainers at all times
- ◆ Send copies of any written material produced by participants to each participant after the course. If you include course material in reports make sure you acknowledge where it comes from

Training to perfection – a case study

I recently attended a two-day workshop on changing days. Although I was a bit sceptical when I received the invitation, my manager sat down with me and explained how this workshop fitted into the whole programme of change and why I needed to go. At the workshop I was surprised by the different backgrounds that people came from. Some people had a lot more experience than me. The workshop was a good mix between group work and presentations. The trainer paced the work so that we all had more than enough to do, but we all got to finish each task before we moved on to the next. I was impressed that the trainer was able to say he had as much clue about what to do as we did about some things. However, I felt reassured that what I had to say was important and I was listened to. Yesterday, I got a copy of the feedback and the written work we did in the groups. It was good to get the feedback as it reminded me about what I had learned on the course and what I had said I would do. Best of all, I didn't get a chance to add to my doodle collection.

A changed participant, July 1997

Training is sometimes seen by organisations as an optional extra, something that can be bought in and forgotten about. However, if an organisation wants to change the way it delivers services, improve quality and be responsive to the needs of service users and carers, training is vital. High quality, diverse training which responds to the needs of the organisation, staff, service users and carers, does not have to cost a great deal of money but it does require commitment and support from all those who believe in changing days.

A training strategy – Getting started

Steps of change	Possible training needs
Create allies: parents, users, employers, senior managers, community organisations. Set up a 'change' group	Training needs analysis for each member of staff
Sharing values; bring people together to create desire for change, ask what's desirable and undesirable about services. What does an 'ideal' future look like?	Values training; social role valorisation. New ways of working; supporting one person at a time. Recognise the need for practical skills. Make sure staff have the confidence to carry out new tasks
Develop skills in person-centred planning, Circles of Support. Complete a person-centred plan for everyone	Person-centred planning training. How to do profiles. User training to participate in and respond to person-centred plans
Use person-centred plan results to understand future needs and wants	Training for users and staff in community participation, community bridge building and community development
Stakeholders' conference: present information from person-centred plans and information on what's desirable, undesirable and ideal	Identify and respond to any team development issues. Offer opportunities for stress management
Create a blueprint for the future. Produce a strategy. Increase supported employment, small businesses, individualise support, set up direct payments	Training for all in direct payments. Users: choosing your own support worker. Staff: supporting individuals to manage direct payments, running small businesses, job coaching, college coaching, etc.
Consultation on strategy	Reassess training needs and make sure that training continues to be available after the initial period of change is completed

Chapter 18

Transport

Vision and Principles

Gaining access to private and public transport is central to increasing people's choices, making their lifestyle more varied and improving the overall quality of their lives. Unless transport issues are really taken seriously, people using services will probably be restricted in what they can do and where they can go.

Flexible provision of transport and giving everyone comprehensive travel training are essential building blocks in a new, more community-based service.

Transport requirements should be included in a person's individual plan and specified in their community care assessment.

Direct payments will help achieve flexible purchasing by service users or carers.

Special transport can segregate and stigmatise people unnecessarily. Rather than help them join the community, it marks them out and separates them further from the general public.

Public transport must be redesigned to make it easier to use for people with learning difficulties. This means making the vehicles and services easy to identify with predictable stops and constant indications that show where the bus is and what the next stop will be.

All transport services should be designed so that people with learning difficulties can understand the published information – especially about routes and timetables – as well as the way in which the services work on the street. Thought also needs to be given to ticketing systems, route planning and bus stop design.

Transport purchasers and providers need to work with public transport authorities to make services realistically available for people with learning difficulties. ■

The publication *Changing Days* set out some of the bad practice which is still unfortunately common two years on and also included detailed suggestions about transport. Here we repeat briefly some of the good ideas and report on information gained over the past two years. Substantial contributions for this chapter come from two pieces of research.

The first explores ways of meeting user needs through innovative transport approaches and is work currently in progress at the Centre for Transport Studies, University College, London. The second is research commissioned by Ely Hospital as part of their Changing Days work.[1] This explored systems that enable people to use individualised transport and travel within Cardiff and elsewhere in the UK.

A flexible transport policy

People want transport that meets their needs. This can only happen by having a range of options available. Transport policy therefore has to be more flexible at the local level. Such transport policy will include the following features:

- vehicles being bought at unit manager or practitioner level or by the service user or carer
- transport planning groups that involve service users and carers, community transport and bus company representatives and independent transport specialists
- travel training tailored to each individual's level of ability and activities, such as how to get to work, the swimming pool or the shops
- flexibility that enables someone to start their journey from home rather than have to go to the day centre first
- talks with local voluntary organisations and carers' groups to establish transport provision under contract.

Using service transport differently

As *Changing Days* said, it is difficult to create more flexible lifestyles if services are trapped in a block transport contract which preserves the 'there and back again' ride to a day centre. Two years on, this is still the only option for many people with learning difficulties. Transport should be available where, when and how people require it. Evening and weekend travel is important but special transport is often not available at these times or is oversubscribed or very expensive.

In order to overcome these difficulties, some areas have reorganised their existing transport resources. One approach is to co-ordinate the use of vehicles from different transport providers – social services, health authority and community transport, for example.

In Devon,[2] considerable sums have been saved and greater cost-effectiveness achieved by centralising control of the fleet. Thus a health authority user could be travelling in a social services department vehicle. This has resulted in better use of vehicles and a reduction in trip costs. Transport partnerships are also being developed that operate in relatively small geographical areas and create local, flexible transport facilities while promoting efficient sharing of vehicles and no duplication of services.

Kent County Council[3] operates a transport service which combines the needs of education, public bus users and health and social services users. Initially, two buses were allocated: one ran a local bus service and the other carried school children for public services in the early morning, then took people with an escort to hospital for social services, reverting to a local bus service in the middle of the day. The process was reversed in the afternoon. Following the success of this experiment, a third bus was obtained to provide social services transport to a day centre for adults with learning disabilities. This flexible use of the vehicles has resulted in large cost savings and has provided accessible transport for villages which had not had bus services for many years.

West Norfolk wanted to make the best use of voluntary sector and statutory transport fleets to provide a more flexible service for elderly and disabled people in rural communities. The West Norfolk Community Transport Project was set up in 1993 and run by a committee of district council, county council social services, voluntary sector and health authority representatives. It employs a full-time manager/co-ordinator, two full-time and two part-time drivers supplemented by a pool of around 100 volunteer drivers. The main client is social services but part of the co-ordinator's brief is to encourage other groups with their own transport to join in. The benefits of increased income, cheaper servicing, access to a pool of volunteer drivers and assistance with legal, financial and safety matters are essential in encouraging other voluntary groups to join the system.

People with learning difficulties can and do make use of these services even though they are not specifically designed for them. The main benefit is that by using available vehicles more effectively, costs are kept under control and providing more comprehensive services becomes more realistic.

Another approach that provides even greater flexibility is being tried in the London Borough of Hackney. This is being set up as a transport co-ordination centre to combine all the available services and vehicles in a single resource. One of its main aims will be to provide transport so that people can travel without planning ahead. The problem at the time of writing is how to change from the current provider-controlled 'bulk service' system to a user-controlled flexible service without incurring a loss of service in the meantime. This is a problem of organisation rather than operation, but it is extremely important to ensure that the changeover is smooth.

Individual purchasing and leasing schemes

More and more people are now purchasing or leasing their own vehicles using mobility allowances and other personal savings, sometimes combined with other money. The vehicle may be for the use of one person or bought by two or three people in one house pooling their resources. At Ely Hospital a vehicle was bought for one ward by pooling the resources of the people living on that ward.

The Cardiff research shows that while these schemes undoubtedly improve quality of life, they are not without problems.

- Insurance costs are high, typically around £600 per year per vehicle
- Most policies stipulate that drivers must be over 25 years old but many small residential schemes employ younger people
- Many of these young staff don't drive and services seldom assist with driving lessons
- Services are reluctant to pay the additional insurance premiums for staff who use their own vehicles
- The fact that limited or no mobility allowance is paid to people who are not physically disabled but whose behaviour prevents them from using public transport makes it harder for them to take part in community activities

Services need to consider these points if they are to provide a transport system which reflects the needs of *all* the clients they serve.

Staff training

Staff training is a key element. Bus drivers and others with direct public contact must have disability awareness training which includes how to help people use travel passes or pay the fare, know where they are and where they need to go. Attention could be given to crew rostering so that, for instance, the same bus crews can be recognised on the same services. Greater Manchester Passenger Transport Executive[4] is an example of good practice in this respect. In addition, people with learning difficulties in Greater Manchester are issued with bus passes which have a green border. This indicates to the driver that the holder might need particular attention but without being obviously identifiable to the general public.

Learning how to travel

In order for someone to successfully complete a journey, they must be able to manage every part of it, door to door. So if any part of that journey is obstructed it makes the whole venture impossible; this includes being able to read timetables and route plans as well as the ability to use buses, pay the fare and so on.

Travel training can be taught in stages, not all of which need involve actual travelling on mainstream public transport services. For example, people can start by learning to travel on a less segregated – but still specialised – service. They learn to make a journey independently but within a more sympathetic environment than the 'real world'. They can then progress to using a public transport service with appropriate support and as confidence increases, eventually travel on their own.

This training cannot be done without the co-operation of the local bus operator, who must be able to understand what is being taught and play a large part in the exercise.

To provide the resources necessary for such training could be prohibitively expensive, particularly when the existing transport fleet is not being run cost-effectively. The co-ordination schemes mentioned earlier could provide a solution which would allow vehicles to be used in this way. However, the trainers must be properly resourced so that the appropriate amount of supervision can be given. This should not be underestimated.

Travel training should include:

- planning the journey
- finding the bus stop
- waiting in the queue
- recognising the right bus
- stopping the bus with a hand signal
- boarding the bus
- showing bus pass or paying the fare
- finding an empty seat and sitting down
- recognising when to get ready to get off
- getting up and ringing the bell
- getting off at the right stop
- being able to do the journey in both directions

The Hackney Plus Bus

IN THE LONDON BOROUGH OF Hackney a pilot scheme funded by the Bridge House Estates Trust Fund is operating the Plus Bus service specifically for mobility-impaired people. It runs on a fixed route and to a timetable. The route is designed to serve places that potential users said they would like to be able to travel to. The drivers and other staff are all trained in disability awareness. So the service falls somewhere between a conventional bus route and the door-to-door services such as Dial-a-Ride and taxis.

The reliable scheduled service provides people with the ability to make choices – about their travel time, destination and the activities they want to do. For the first time, people can choose to visit a day centre for a short time and then go to the shops before returning home rather than have to wait for the 'milk-round' bus to collect them for the homeward trip. This provides not just transport – it provides choices. The intention is to establish a network of similar services in the borough to link with conventional public transport services.

All the information about the service, including route (Figure 1) and timetable (Figure 2), is designed to make it easy to understand. Each area through which the bus passes is identified by a different symbol – a pictogram of a tree or a bird, for example. These appear in all published information and inside the bus itself on an illuminated display panel. As the bus travels along the route, the place name and the pictogram light up to show where the bus is and what the next stop will be. The project is still at an experimental stage and the designs of the pictograms are still to be finalised. ∎

Place		Time	
Homerton Hospital	**H** HOMERTON	(clock)	09:00
Linzell Estate	LINZELL	(clock)	09:05
Sorsby Health Centre	(figure icon)	(clock)	09:10
Chatsworth Road	CHATS WORTH	(clock)	09:15
Athena Health Centre	(figure icon)	(clock)	09:20
Mare Street shops	MARE STREET	(clock)	09:30
Nightingale Flats	(bird icon)	(clock)	09:40
Lower Clapton Health Centre	(figure icon)	(clock)	09:50
Homerton Hospital	**H** HOMERTON	(clock)	10:00

Figure 1 Hackney Plusbus Timetable

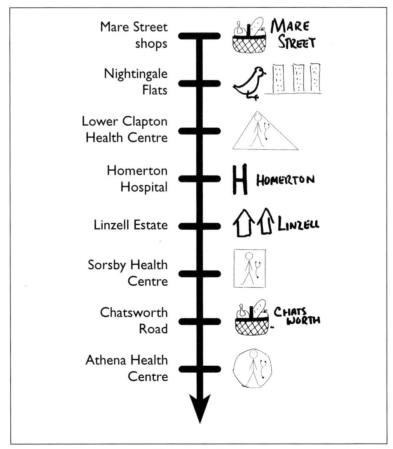

Figure 2 Route

References

1. Mitchell P. *Changing Days: Initial transport research and UK transport research.* Cardiff: Welsh Centre for Learning disabilities Applied Research, 1997.
2. Brown NLCK. *Case Study: Operation of Transport Co-ordination Centres.* London: University of London Centre for Transport Studies Working Paper. University of London, 1997 (unpublished).
3. *Ibid.*
4. Barber E, Hajnrych J. Use of public transport by people with learning difficulties. *Proceedings of PTRC Summer Annual Meeting, Seminar on Transport for People with Mobility Handicaps.* London: London Borough of Hackney. Planning & Transport, Research & Consultancy, 1993.

Further reading

Taylor J. Co-ordination of Accessible Transport Services. *Proceedings of PTRC Summer Annual Meeting, Seminar on Transport for People with Mobility Handicaps.* London: London Borough of Hackney, 1993.

Profile poster

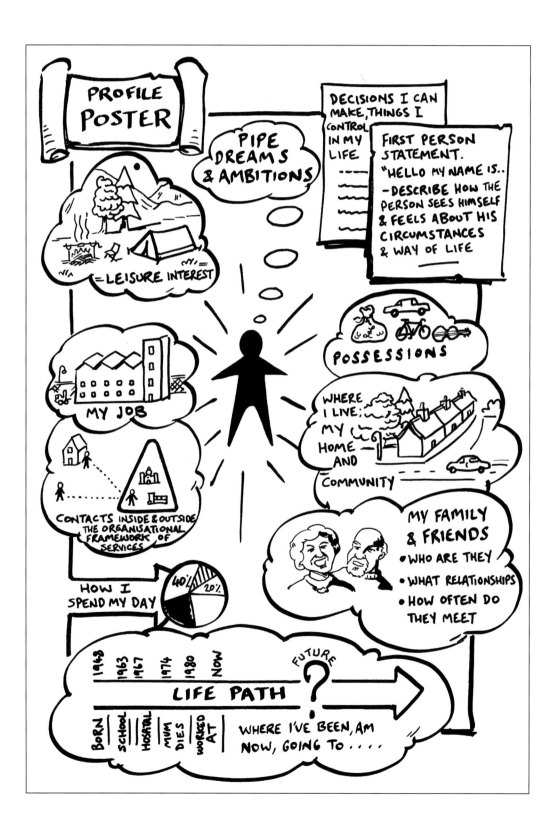

Appendix 2

A roadmap for development

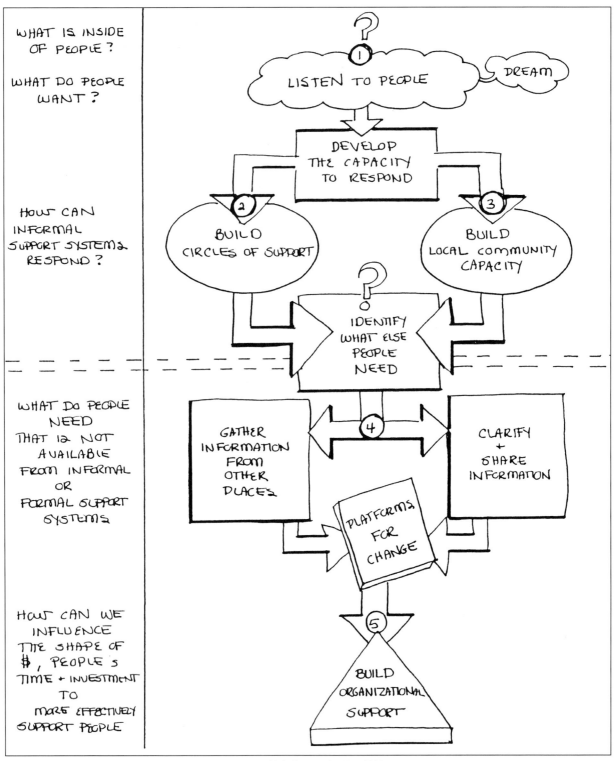

WHAT IS INSIDE
OF PEOPLE?

WHAT DO PEOPLE
WANT?

? ① LISTEN TO PEOPLE — DREAM

DEVELOP
THE CAPACITY
TO RESPOND

HOW CAN
INFORMAL
SUPPORT SYSTEMS
RESPOND?

② BUILD CIRCLES OF SUPPORT

③ BUILD LOCAL COMMUNITY CAPACITY

? ○ IDENTIFY WHAT ELSE PEOPLE NEED

WHAT DO PEOPLE
NEED
THAT IS NOT
AVAILABLE
FROM INFORMAL
OR
FORMAL SUPPORT
SYSTEMS

④

GATHER
INFORMATION
FROM
OTHER
PLACES

CLARIFY + SHARE INFORMATION

PLATFORMS FOR CHANGE

HOW CAN WE
INFLUENCE
THE SHAPE OF
$, PEOPLE's
TIME + INVESTMENT
TO
MORE EFFECTIVELY
SUPPORT PEOPLE

⑤ BUILD ORGANIZATIONAL SUPPORT

Source: Mount B *et al. Person-centered Development.* Manchester (CT): Communitas Inc., 1991.

Day opportunities

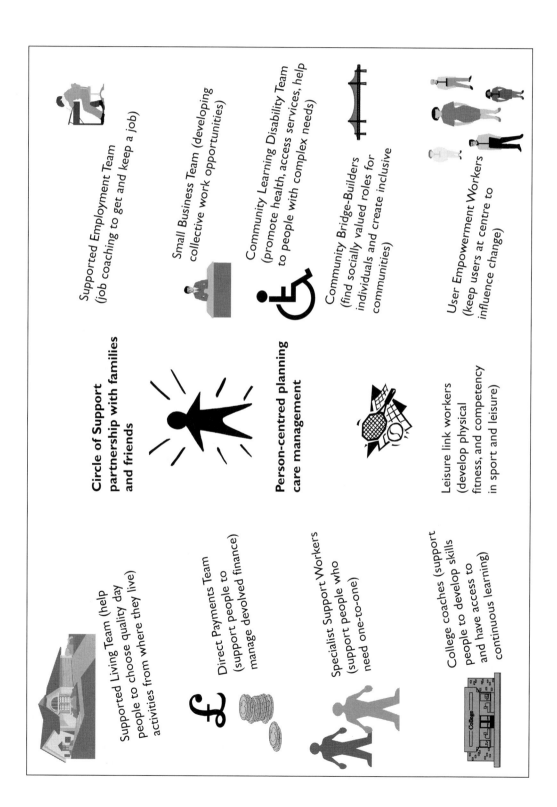

Supported Employment Team (job coaching to get and keep a job)

Small Business Team (developing collective work opportunities)

Community Learning Disability Team (promote health, access services, help to people with complex needs)

Community Bridge-Builders (find socially valued roles for individuals and create inclusive communities)

User Empowerment Workers (keep users at centre to influence change)

Circle of Support partnership with families and friends

Person-centred planning care management

Leisure link workers (develop physical fitness, and competency in sport and leisure)

Supported Living Team (help people to choose quality day activities from where they live)

Direct Payments Team (support people to manage devolved finance)

Specialist Support Workers (support people who need one-to-one)

College coaches (support people to develop skills and have access to and continuous learning)

Extract from Cardiff Community Access Officers' Operational Policy

Mission statement

To adhere to the principles of the All Wales Strategy, in that every person with a learning disability (and their carers) should have access to a comprehensive range of community-based opportunities, planned to meet their identified needs.

To enable the individual with a learning disability to be less dependent on specialist services and, over time, become an integral member of his/her local community, including mutual and long-lasting relationships.

Aims

- To establish 'whole life' patterns of provision that are based on the interests of one person, not determined or restricted by any service supports. Any opportunities 'set-up' will be community-based and aimed to maximise involvement with people who live and work locally.

- To work with individuals, 'supporters' and advocates, in order to enable access to:
  - community facilities
  - community groups
  - ordinary community-based opportunities
  - social networks.

- To work with community members and general public facilities and service providers to enable access to the above.

Objectives

- To facilitate access to the full range of information potentially relevant to an individual need.
- To provide a specialist assessment, looking specifically at what might be preventing a

person from accessing normal patterns of living – leisure, education, occupation and social networks.

- To assist 'planners' and 'supporters' of individuals to look in detail at a person's social network and to facilitate approaches which aim to increase community involvement, inclusion and participation.
- To work with community members and general public facility and service providers to overcome obstacles to opportunity. For example, poor attitude (lack of awareness), bad physical access, lack of active equal opportunity policy.
- To encourage best possible use of 'in-house' resources and systems in order to enable the taking up of opportunities.
- To form links with community members and groups of current or potential significance to individuals. To seek opportunities via this 'network'.

Reason(s) for referral (criteria)

A person should have 'targets', as identified by their Community Care Assessment (CAO), which relate directly to the 'objectives' of the CAOs, as outlined in this policy.

Access officers should be included in every stage of an individual's planning process, working alongside Community Care Managers and other personnel as necessary.

Use of budget

The CAO budget is to be used in the following ways:

- To fund 'taster' sessions
- Funding towards a 'pilot' project
- Initial funding for capital equipment/stock within a new initiative
- Equipment, training and travel costs, as needed for the CAO, to fulfil the daily requirements of their work
- Funding for one-off pieces of work, undertaken by community groups, on behalf of a CAO.

NB: The budget is not available to provide on-going support for a regular activity.

Moving on

Community Access Officers aim to identify opportunities that offer potential from which individuals may progress into more integrated settings, encouraging more networking with local communities. Whether this actually occurs is often dependent upon the support an individual receives and we work closely with supporters to encourage good practice and promote approaches which maximise an individual's chances of success.

Volunteers

Community Access Officers work alongside voluntary agencies to promote the involvement of clients in as wide a range of activities as possible; this includes clients taking on the role of a volunteer in their own right.

We do not have a policy for enrolling our own volunteers, but we can work alongside other agencies to assist them in developing networks of volunteers to support or work alongside our clients.

South Glamorgan Social Services – job description (extract) – community access officer (resettlement)

Main purpose of the job

1. To work with people with learning difficulties who are due to or have been resettled by the Resettlement Team.

   – with the particular responsibility to identify or create access to community facilities and social networks, leading to – less dependence on 'service support' systems and developing in their place a 'self support' network of friends and associates within the person's neighbourhood.

Aims

1. To work with service users, house staff and others so as to enable service users to make informed CHOICES about accessing community facilities and social networks.

2. To work with service users, house staff and others so as to enable service users to express their INDIVIDUALITY in accessing community facilities and social networks.

3. To work with service users, house staff and others so as to enable clients not only to BE PRESENT but to PARTICIPATE in their community.

4. To work with service users, house staff and others so as to enable service users to gain STATUS and RESPECT within their community.

5. To work with service users, house staff and others so as to enable service users to experience CONTINUITY of place, activity and relationships.

Person specification – Community Access Officer

1. Show an attitude towards people with learning difficulties which is informed by the philosophy underpinning service provision.

2. The ability to present people with learning difficulties as valued community members.

3. The ability to inspire action and ideas in others.

4. Have imagination and ability to translate new ideas into practice.

5. Ability to seek out resources/opportunities in order to match them to individual needs.

6. Have knowledge of the local area.

7. Be able to evaluate and monitor the effectiveness of opportunities.

8. Ability to overcome obstacles.

9. Must have good interpersonal skills.

10. Understanding of and ability to work within different agencies and teams

11. An ability to respond flexibly to the workload and ability to work within an environment of change.

12. To be able to manage own time effectively.

13. The ability to manage a budget.

14. To be literate and numerate.

15. Desirable to be a car driver.

Objectives

1. To ensure the availability to service users and house staff of a comprehensive community profile covering the immediate locality in detail, and the wider community (town, borough), augmenting as necessary the information available from Community Education, Library, Leisure and Amenities Departments, voluntary organisations and other relevant agencies.

2. To participate in individual planning so as to assist service users in identifying and pursuing goals which access them to community facilities and social networks

3. To identify opportunities for access, and work to overcome obstacles (physical, attitudinal, support needs) and avoid saturation with other devalued groups.

4. To introduce new experiences at a pace which enables service users to succeed.

5. To maintain continuing exchange of communication with service users and house staff relating to organisation and routines, including appropriate forms of monitoring and reporting service users' experience of satisfaction and meaningful change.

6. To offer advice to house staff on negotiating and maintaining access and where necessary taking the lead on their behalf.

7. To offer support to staff in their understanding of the role they are expected to perform and the specific goals service users are working to fulfil in accessing community facilities and social networks.

8. To form links with other community services providing information about or support for, community access and where appropriate co-operating with them.

9. To form links with community members of current or potential significance to service users so as to promote acceptance and increase opportunities for access.

10. Where necessary, to develop innovative opportunities for community access.

11. To liaise with those involved in the development of an Employment Strategy in assisting service users to obtain work or work experience, and where necessary, referring service users to the specialists for support.

12. To promote services which reflect ordinary patterns of life – that is enabling people to experience opportunities at appropriate times of the day, week and year. In particular, work and education should be seen most frequently as part of a working week and social/leisure activities during evenings and weekends.

Appendix 6

Risk assessment checklist[*]

Taking measured risk is essential to help people develop new skills and enjoy life to the full.
(Chapter 13)

Developing inclusion requires sensible but flexible risk policies which don't inhibit
someone's opportunities for new relationships and experiences. (Chapter 6)

Below is an example of a risk assessment checklist which may be useful in developing your own policy around risk-taking. Please also refer to Chapters 6 and 13 for more suggestions about risk issues.

1)   Transport/travel risks

i)   Think about mounting/dismounting vehicles

ii)   Think about standing/walking in trains/buses

iii)   Where in the vehicle is the person seated? Who/what is around/close to them, any sharp/dangerous objects, slippery floor surfaces?

iv)   How long will the journey be?

v)   At what time is the journey taking place (e.g. will it be during rush hour with a service user who becomes very distressed in crowds?)?

vi)   Is the person appropriately dressed to travel? Not likely to be too hot or cold?

vii)   If using a wheelchair, is the person properly strapped in?

viii)   If someone needs to be lifted (e.g. to transfer them from a chair to a vehicle), are there enough staff to facilitate proper lifting? Are they being correctly lifted?

ix)   Does the service user understand road safety? How much?

x)   Consider your route. Are there any dangerous main roads to cross – is this a problem? How much walking will there be? Are there any badly made roads/ pavements which could cause someone to fall? Is the walk uphill with someone who will find this a struggle?

xi)   Are there extreme weather conditions such as severe ice on the pavements which is likely to cause an accident?

xii)   Consider any known incidents of previous road traffic accidents, what were the circumstances?

---

* Hackney Independent Living Team, Richmond House, 1a Westgate Street, London E8 3RL

2) Physical harm to self/others

i) Are there any known environmental triggers to the person's behaviour present?

ii) Are there any sharp/heavy objects in the vicinity which could be used to harm someone?

iii) Are there any situations when your hands will be full or the person will be out of your sight – could these times present a danger?

iv) Are there strategies in place for working with harmful behaviours and do you feel able to implement them?

v) Is the service user likely to antagonise members of the public and potentially become physically vulnerable because of their behaviour in the community?

3) Risks within specific activities

i) Are there materials which are used in this activity which could be dangerous (e.g. objects which someone may swallow, sharp objects, hot things)?

ii) Is there adequate support available to facilitate the activity?

iii) Are there any health/medication considerations which could mean that certain aspects of an activity may be unsuitable for the person?

iv) Is the person suitably dressed for the activity?

v) Where is the setting of the activity (e.g. is it held in a large, open area which could present problems for someone who absconds, or is there a fire hazard in the building)?

vi) Are there any triggers in the activity/activity environment which cause upset or unusual behaviours in the individual?

vii) Who will be involved in the activity? Is the service user potentially at risk from any of these people or vice-versa?

viii) Is the activity realistic, can the service user realistically achieve the objectives of the activity?

4) Health and hygiene

i) Is food and medication which the service user ingests hygienically prepared and presented, i.e. are implements used clean, are your hands/the service user's hands clean?

ii) Is food and medication being properly stored (e.g. you are going out for a picnic, are sandwiches properly wrapped and medication stored separately at the right temperature)?

iii) Are you aware of any allergies/conditions that the person has which affects what they can eat (e.g. diabetes)?

iv) Are you aware of specific preparations which the food may require (e.g. food needs to be mashed or very soft so that the person does not choke)?

v) Do you have clear understanding of the medication that the person is receiving, i.e. what it is for, side-effects and exactly how and when it should be administered?

vi) When planning an activity, have you included adequate arrangements for the person to eat (if the activity is at a time that requires this) and to receive their medication?

vii) If the person suffers from conditions such as epilepsy, are you aware of what to do in the event of that person having a fit when out with you? Do any activities trigger/worsen the condition e.g. a venue where there are flashing lights which can affect someone with epilepsy?

viii) Can you adequately perform basic first aid skills if needed?

5) General

i) Is there adequate staff/other support to enable the facilitation of the activity?

ii) Are there any health and safety risks present such as sharp objects/slippery surfaces, fire risks?

iii) Do you have access to emergency numbers which you may need to use (e.g. management numbers, number for the family/next of kin, GP, local police station)?

iv) Do you feel able to adequately support a service user who displays challenging behaviour?

v) Does the service user have ID (either with them or held by you) which could be used if the person went missing?

Profile extracts

The following pages give extracts from profiles used by the Changing Days sites. In the main, the content of the profiles is similar and all use phrasing which keeps the focus on the person as an individual.

Here we have selected sections which together make up various areas of a profile which it is important to consider in developing your own profiling process.

Cambridge

The way the Cambridge questions are phrased is particularly helpful in focusing on the individual. Here is their section on emotional needs.

Emotional needs

Things that help me feel happy and secure are ...

When I feel insecure I ...

Things that frighten me are ...

Things that help me relax if I'm feeling anxious are ...

If I'm feeling sad I like to ...

My most important possessions are ...

My happiest memories are of ...

Hackney

Personal details in Hackney's assessment form include:

Age; Sex; Religion; Race; Languages spoken and understood; Emergency contact; Doctor; Advocate; Address; Tel. No.; Benefits (to check whether the person is getting full entitlement); Money (amount available to spend on community activities).

The form also makes good use of pictures and symbols. Here is the section on communication.

Communication.

How do you communicate to others? How do others make themselves understood by you?

Cardiff

The Cardiff profile includes the important aspect of ideas for future action. The following sections on relationships and being part of the community demonstrate this.

Relationships

Promoting relationships:
List what ideas there are to promote the individual's relationships: e.g. by continuing with the ones that are important to the individual; re-establishing previous contacts; and creating opportunities for new relationships in the individual's network.

Assistance:
What should people know and do to support the individual in building relationships, e.g. support and back-up offered to protect their safety and health, issues concerning their money, how the individual communicates, etc.

Being part of the community

Promoting participating in the community:
What ideas are there to promote the individual's participation in the community: e.g. by continuing with the places and activities that are familiar and important to the individual; revisiting previous places and activities within communities (possibly of origin); increasing the number and regularity of other community settings that the individual would find interesting to use.

Assistance:
What should people know and do to support the individual in participating in the community. Supports and back-ups offered to protect their safety and health; issues concerning (e.g. money, how the person communicates, etc.).

Belfast

The Belfast workbook layout provides plenty of space (for adding drawings, photos or other visual material). Questions are on the left-hand page, with space for answers on the facing page. It also has blank pages between each question.

We reproduce below the whole text of the workbook. Figure 1 opposite shows some sample pages.

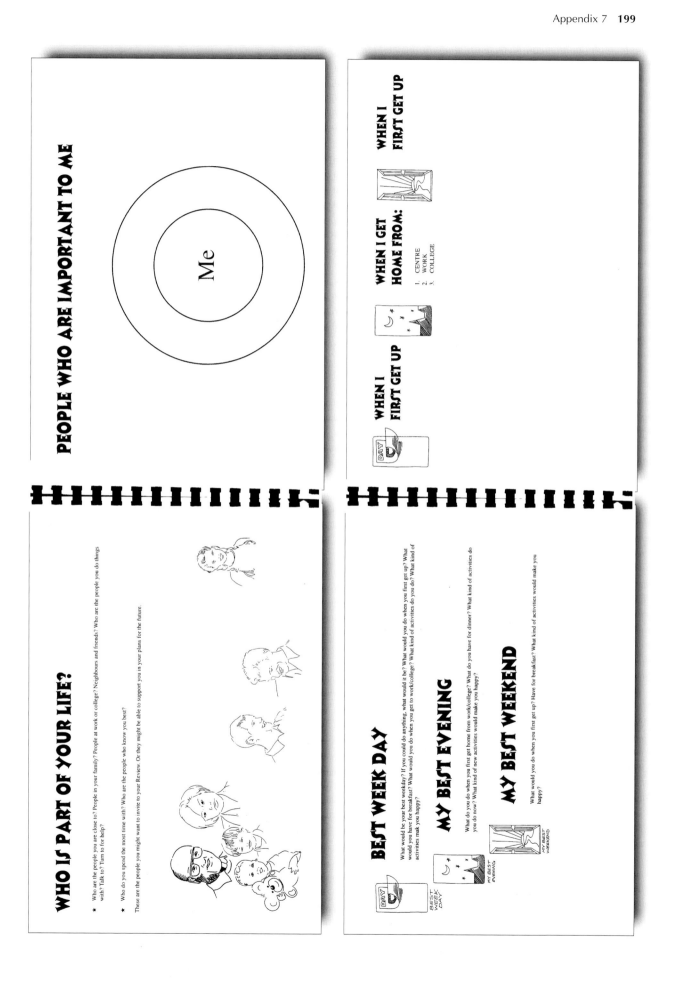

PEOPLE WHO ARE IMPORTANT TO ME

Me

WHO IS PART OF YOUR LIFE?

★ Who are the people you are close to? People in your family? People at work or college? Neighbours and friends? Who are the people you do things with? Talk to? Turn to for help?

★ Who do you spend the most time with? Who are the people who know you best?

These are the people you might want to invite to your Review. Or they might be able to support you in your plans for the future.

WHEN I FIRST GET UP

WHEN I GET HOME FROM:

1. CENTRE
2. WORK
3. COLLEGE

WHEN I FIRST GET UP

BEST WEEK DAY

What would be your best weekday? If you could do anything, what would it be? What would you do when you first get up? What would you have for breakfast? What would you do when you get to work/college? What kind of activities do you do? What kind of activities make you happy?

MY BEST EVENING

What do you do when you first get home from work/college? What do you have for dinner? What kind of activities do you do now? What kind of new activities would make you happy?

MY BEST WEEKEND

What would you do when you first get up? Have for breakfast? What kind of activities would make you happy?

THIS WORKBOOK BELONGS TO ....

WHAT THIS WORKBOOK IS ABOUT

In this workbook, you will have a chance to think about your life and the kinds of things that are important to you. The information can be used to help build your Individual Support Plan. On each page you will find a question and some words about what it means. It's best to do this workbook with people who know and care about you.

Here are some things to think about when you're completing your workbook:

* Invite people who know and care about you (friends, relatives, day care worker, residential worker) to meet with you and help you fill out the workbook.

* Ask the person who was writing things down to go over them with you to make sure that everything is just like you want it.

WHO IS PART OF YOUR LIFE?

* Who are the people you are close to? People in your family? People at work or college? Neighbours and friends? Who are the people you do things with? Talk to? Turn to for help?

* Who do you spend the most time with? Who are the people who know you best?

These are the people you might want to invite to your review. Or they might be able to support you in your plans for the future.

PEOPLE WHO ARE IMPORTANT TO ME

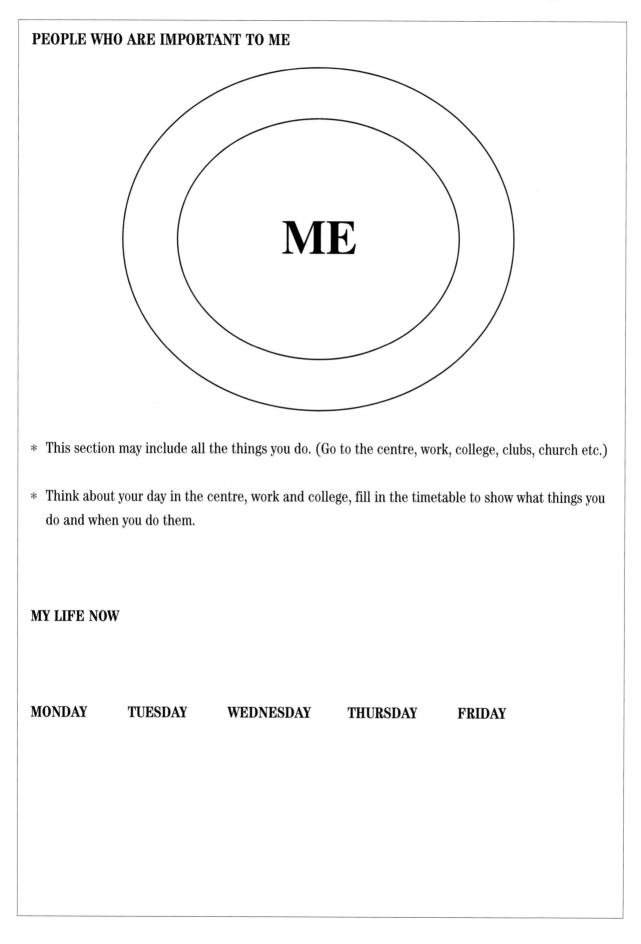

ME

* This section may include all the things you do. (Go to the centre, work, college, clubs, church etc.)

* Think about your day in the centre, work and college, fill in the timetable to show what things you do and when you do them.

MY LIFE NOW

MONDAY	TUESDAY	WEDNESDAY	THURSDAY	FRIDAY

WHAT ARE SOME GOOD THINGS ABOUT YOU?

What do you like about yourself? What are you good at? Proud of? What nice things do people say about you? What do people thank you for? This is sometimes hard for people to answer. So you might want to start by asking a friend or relative.

These are important things to think about when you are thinking about the kinds of services and supports you need and want.

WHAT THINGS DO YOU LIKE TO DO?

What things do you like to do? At home? At college? For fun? Around town? On holiday? What kind of music do you like? What kind of films do you like? What kind of food do you like? Do you have any hobbies? Do you belong to any groups or clubs? Do you collect things?

WHAT THINGS DO YOU NOT LIKE?

What things do you not like to do at home? At work? At college? What kinds of food do you not like? What kinds of things annoy/upset you?

What kinds of things make you angry, sad, annoyed?

BEST WEEK DAY

What would be your best weekday? If you could do anything, what would it be? What would you do when you first get up? What would you have for breakfast? What would you do when you get to work/college? What kind of activities do you do? What kind of activities make you happy?

MY BEST EVENING

What do you do when you first get home from work/college? What do you have for dinner? What kind of activities do you do now? What kind of new activities make you happy?

MY BEST WEEKEND

What would you do when you first get up? Have for breakfast? What kind of activities would make you happy?

WHAT IS IMPORTANT TO ME

Look back at the things you wrote down or said when we talked about who is important in your life, things you like to do, your best day, evening, weekend.

What is most important for us to remember? What things do you want to make sure are in your life every day (like a cup of coffee in the morning, or a favourite friend)? What things do you want to make sure are *not* in your life every day (like a certain kind of music or some food you can't stand)?

ARE THERE OTHER THINGS WE NEED TO KNOW OR DO TO SUPPORT YOU?

Are there things we haven't talked about that would help us support you? For example, are there things we need to know or do to support your health? Are there certain medicines you take? Are there certain physical things that you should or should not do? Are there certain things we need to know or do to make sure you stay safe? Are there thing we need to know about the food that you eat? Are there things that make you upset that we need to know about?

WHAT IS IMPORTANT TO ME

Are there things you would like to be able to do but that you don't have the opportunity to do i.e. swimming, work placement, college, watch a particular programme etc.

Are there things that you would like to do but need special help/support?

Index